P9-CQX-815

MARXISM AND HISTORY

Helmut Fleischer

Marxism and History

Translated by Eric Mosbacher

Harper & Row, Publishers
New York, Evanston, San Francisco, London

Contents

Preface

Trying to define the position of Marxist philosophy, particularly the Marxist philosophy of history that is to be discussed here, means entering a highly controversial field. In view of the diversity of the theoretical and practical work of its founders, who did not devote the whole of their lives to the development of a philosophical system, and the multiformity of later forms of 'Marxism', clarity in the matter is not so easily attained. Nevertheless it should be possible by means of systematic interpretation and systematic evaluation to arrive at a closer definition, and in particular to rule out certain things that are certainly not Marxist. The present work is intended to be a contribution to this task. It is not intended to cover the whole ground, but to be merely a systematic survey presenting a number of corrections and refutations – some of them categorical, others more hypothetical in nature. The choice of subject and the selection of texts quoted was to a large extent dictated by a critical look at current interpretations of Marxism. My original intention was merely to draw up an interim balance-sheet of the state of the discussion of Marxist philosophy in the German-speaking world (ten years after that drawn up in 1957 by J. Habermas), but I then decided on a greater concentration of subject-matter.

The present study forms part of the very intensive efforts being made at the present time to reconstruct Marxist philosophy as a humanist-emancipatory philosophy of practice. The attempt that is made here to establish history as a dimension of human practice is intended to contrast in particular with two developments of the Marxist concept of history which – based on different approaches to the problem by the founders of Marxism

– have hitherto dominated debate on the subject. From one of these – the early writings of 1844 – a general anthropological definition of the meaning of history has been deduced; history is presented as a process directed towards man's becoming fully man in the whole wealth of his being, harmoniously united with his like and with a nature that has been humanized, though by way of the negativity of 'alienation'. The other, based on the *Critique of Political Economy*, has given rise to a highly material and sober view of history as a process of correlative development of productive forces and productive relations governed by the objective laws of a logic of social relations uninfluenced by human intentions. This latter view of history has become dominant in the historical materialism of the Soviet school, and with its logic of structures and processes sometimes reaches such a degree of abstraction that it is possible to say of it – as Marx said of Hobbes – that materialism has here become 'anti-human'. It is in reaction against this anti-humanism that the 'young' and 'humanist' Marx has been resurrected, but humanism tends to lead easily to sentimentalization and theoretical aberration and to end up in sterile talk about alienation and man's 'true nature'.

The *Theses on Feuerbach* and other writings of 1845–6 on the materialist view of history put forward a view of historical 'practice' that is both self-critically directed against the earlier ideas of 1844 and sets critical limits to the later references to the laws underlying historical processes. We are faced here, not just with a provisional formulation of what Marx stated in 'classical' form in his *Critique of Political Economy*, but with one of the foundations of Marxist historical thought. There is justification for seeking a better understanding of the 'later' and 'mature' Marx from the study of the 'young' Marx, but one should not solely and excessively concentrate on the author of the *Paris Manuscripts* of 1844, but take into account above all the Marx and Engels of the criticism of Feuerbach.

The first of the five chapters is concerned with examining what Marx and Engels wrote on the theory of history. This, in the author's view, yields three different approaches – to the meaning of history as a whole, the way it works in practice, and its underlying laws. The next three chapters are more specifically concerned with the problems arising from these approaches.

In the one dealing with its 'driving forces' we have above all to explain the concept of history as practice, history-making activity and its subjective centre. The chapter on the totality of the historical process is devoted to the question of the general meaning of history, which was very prominent on Marx's and Engels's horizon in 1844, though it then receded from their field of vision without ever completely disappearing from it. In the chapter on historical necessity we discuss some of the key problems that arise from attempting to organize history into an objective logical system. The last chapter discusses very selectively some problems of the Marxist interpretation of contemporary history.

One Approaches to a Marxist Theory of History

From the very beginning 'history' has been a key word in Marxist philosophy – in the sense that a great deal is locked up in it; so much so that trying to unlock it has become one of the hazards of the modern history of ideas. Even after a whole century of interpretation and system-building, our picture of Marx's and the Marxist theory is a very uncertain one. When one considers on the one hand, for instance, K. R. Popper's reconstruction of Marxist 'historicism' and on the other the ideas of the contemporary advocates of a 'Marxist humanism', it is clear that there could hardly be greater disagreement than that which has arisen from this attempt to draw conclusions from a fragmentary series of texts.

The nature of the texts themselves is one of the things that makes for such divergence. They are without exception fragmentary, they belong to different phases of their authors' development, and often enough definite aspects of their views are emphasized for polemical purposes. All this has become so topical, however, only because Marx's work has stimulated the enthusiasm and the hatred of the political parties as has hardly anything else in our century.

A distinctive feature of most interpretations is the great self-confidence with which unequivocal and categorical statements are made about the Marxist theory of history, often based on quotations that offer the flimsiest foundation. Many, for instance, have no hesitation in seeing the essence of the theory in a handy phrase coined by one of Marx's reviewers. The polemically accentuated phraseology of the Marxist classics has given critics many opportunities to pin down Marx in extreme and surprising positions. Even where he has been canonized, selective interpretations of his and Engels's works have led to an often very subtle but on the whole gross distortion of the Marxist interpretation of history.

Our survey is intended to contribute to extracting the Marxist concept of history from the straits of such one-sided interpretation, to rescue it from its strangeness and make it more intelligible, and to demonstrate its elasticity and 'experimental' nature instead of its alleged rigidity. A great deal is gained by considering the relevant passages from Marx and Engels in a not too narrow selection, by carefully weighing them up against one another, and using their inner counterpoint, not to draw hasty conclusions, but as the starting-point for more thorough consideration.

Let us begin by taking the bull by the horns. What was Karl Marx's view of history? Some of the relevant passages suggest the existence of a succinct Marxist answer to the question, perhaps on the lines of Hegel's saying that 'world history is progress in consciousness of freedom – the necessity of which we have to recognize' as a 'series of steps in development'. This, though without the accent on 'consciousness', would seem to be Marx's view too, and in fact not a few critics as well as spokesmen of Marxism have regarded it as such. 'To Marx', L. Kofler says, 'history seems to be a series of ever higher steps in human freedom and the self-realization of man.'[1]

But, if we continue our examination of the fragmentary passages on the philosophy of history to be found in Marx and Engels, such generalizations promptly become dubious again. Sometimes it seems as if the idea of a history of the world and of humanity tending to a specific goal has completely vanished, as if to Marx history were not a theodicy but the very odyssey that O. K. Flechtheim describes it as in his attack on Marx.[2]

With a little schematization, several approaches by the founders of Marxism to a concept of history can be discerned.

1. That attributing to it a universal meaning. History is seen as a process of humanization. To the young Marx of 1844 this process was thought of in an ideal sense, as being inherent in the nature of the human species, while in Marx's and Engels's later works the idea is more 'naturalistic', history becomes 'the humanization of the ape', the genesis of a new species.

We may call this the anthropological or anthropogenetic approach.

2. That based on the concrete historical conduct of mankind. History is regarded as the outcome, more blind than the result of any tendency to a specific goal, of the actions of individuals and groups impelled by their needs in the situations in which they find themselves. This we may call the pragmatological approach.

3. The approach based on the logic of objective historical structures and processes. History is here regarded as a natural process taking place in accordance with definite laws. This is the nomological approach.

These different approaches each reveal a different aspect and impose a different accent. They are not mutually exclusive, indeed they are legitimate only to the extent that they complement each other. But it is easy for any one of them to be presented in isolation and to be exaggerated accordingly, or for them to be incompletely combined, with the result that an important corrective is lacking. Many interpretations of the Marxist theory of history suffer from this defect, and in particular the most broadly-based attempt at its systematic development, the historical materialism of the Soviet Marxist school. Before going into individual problems, we shall examine the views on history that result from these different approaches and the tasks that face those who would like to establish a synthesis of the Marxist interpretation of history as a whole.

1. HISTORY AS 'HUMANIZATION'

In 1844, when Marx turned to socialism, he (like Engels) had a very definite idea of man and of human worth as the opposite pole to the 'Philistine world', the 'political animal kingdom'. The Philistines, he wrote to Ruge in 1843, were the lords of the old world; all their society needed was a large number of slaves, and even the slaves did not feel the need of freedom. People of that kind, 'who do not feel themselves to be men, cleave to their masters, like a breed of slaves or horses'. In contrast to this, 'human beings would be creatures with minds, free men, republicans'. But Philistines did not want to be like that. 'Human self-feeling, freedom, would first have to be reawakened in the

breast of these people', for with Christianity and the dis-
appearance of the Greeks from the world it had vanished into
the blue haze of heaven.[3]

To Marx the transition to socialism and communism meant
associating the idea of the emancipation of man with that of the
emancipation of the proletariat and gaining a more complete
understanding of the conditions 'in which man has become a
degraded, enslaved, abandoned and contemptible creature'. At
the same time the idea of human emancipation opened up a
great world historical perspective in Marx's mind. In the *Paris
Manuscripts* of 1844 he gave a significant answer to the question
of what history meant to mankind and its way of being. It was
the realization of an aim imposed on him, the development of
full humanity, of all the potentialities of his nature. But the
idea of a trend to human self-realization at work in history did
not last for long; only a year later he criticized it sharply. But –
in a very different theoretical frame of reference, perhaps – it
reappears in the passage in which Marx gives the 'classical'
description of his view of history, in the preface to the *Critique
of Political Economy* of 1859, where he mentions quite incidentally that all previous history was really only the 'prehistory'
of human society. Accurately establishing the theoretical frame
of reference that now applies is one of the hardest tasks that
confront interpreters of Marxist philosophy. Most of them
have hitherto preferred to associate themselves with the impressive propositions of Marx's early phase and to regard them
as the quintessence of the Marxist philosophy of history. We
think it preferable to discuss the two stages separately.

A. *History as the unification of man's existence and being*

Let us take a glance at the crucial statements on the philosophy
of history in Marx's *Economic-Philosophical Manuscripts*: 'History . . . is a real part of natural history, of nature developing
into man.' The 'whole of so-called world history (is) nothing
but the engendering of man by human labour, natural becoming leading to the production of man'. Thus, 'like everything
natural . . . man too has his act of origin, history. . . . History
is the true natural history of man'. An important dividing line
exists between the 'movement of history . . . that is not yet the

real history of man that is its goal, but is only the act of production, the history of the origin of man', and the real history of man, between the 'society that is becoming' and the 'society that has become'. This – still outstanding – society that has 'become', i.e., has reached the goal of its becoming, 'produces . . . man (in the) whole wealth of his being, man richly and deeply mentally alive, as its permanent reality'.[4]

The historical process of human becoming leads through a negative phase, a phase of alienation. Marx analyses the alienative effects characteristic of capitalist production (alienation between worker and the means of production, the products of his labour and his labour itself; between man and man, man and his species, man and his real nature); but he does not attempt to localize alienated resistance in history as a whole (i.e., demonstrate its historical origin or what preceded it). The important point is that in relation to this alienated existence man's future realization of his nature will take the form of a 'reacquisition', a 'reintegration, or return of man to himself'. Sometimes man's passing through the negative phase of alienated existence seems to have a deeper meaning in relation to the totally positive phase for which it is preparing. When Marx writes: 'The human essence must be reduced to this absolute poverty so that its inner wealth may be born of it',[5] one feels reminded of mythological motivations; a deep necessity seems to be at work, as a result of which the road to the kingdom of heaven runs through a vale of tears.

This future society, we are told, will arise as a result of the communist movement. But at first communism acts in many 'crude' forms, and in reference to this Marx says in one passage: 'Communism is the necessary form and the energetic principle of the immediate future, but communism as such is not the goal of human development, which is the formation of human society.' This phase of communism is still affected by human alienation, but by passing through and beyond it 'the positive elimination of private property as human self-alienation' and thus the real 'acquisition of true human nature through and for men' are attained. Also this communism, that represents the completion of naturalism and humanism, is 'the real solution of the conflict between man and nature and with men, the true abolition of the conflict between existence and being, between objectification and activity of the self, between freedom and necessity, between the individual and the species. It is the solution of the riddle of history and knows itself to be that solution'.[6]

Because of its coherence and confidence, the concept of history of the *Paris Manuscripts* turned out to be very attractive to Marx's interpreters, for it presented history as a 'totality with a definite trend, combining past and future in a living unity'[7], a 'uniform process with a recognizable beginning and an end knowable in advance', a 'goal towards which the endeavours of the whole of humanity in history were directed'.[8] Marx's philosophy of history is described as a 'humanist logodicy' bearing a close resemblance to Hegel's teaching. 'If to Hegel the meaning of world history lies in the self-realization and self-comprehension of the spirit, to the atheist humanism of Feuerbach's pupil it lies in the realization of "total, fully and deeply self-aware man".'[9] Marxism is described as an 'ethical-religious system of thought' and its philosophy of history interprets the latter in accordance with the usual religious pattern of losing and regaining – the lost paradise to be regained in this instance being communism – 'that is the great design of world history as Marx explains it'.[10] 'The whole historical process ... reflects the general pattern of the Judaeo-Christian interpretation of history as a providential process of salvation leading to a meaningful final goal.'[11] All these are possible extrapolations from Marx's fragments of 1844. But the question is whether they can be regarded as an adequate statement of Marx's and Marxist historical thought – and it is precisely this that we dispute. Our whole survey is to be regarded as an attempt to interpret it otherwise. But first of all let us examine the passages in which Marx himself (together with Engels) settled accounts with his 'philosophical conscience' of 1844.

The self-criticism of 1845–6. If there is a break anywhere in his philosophical development, it lies not between the 'young' and 'old' (or 'mature') Marx, but between his twenty-sixth and twenty-eighth years, between the Feuerbach worship of the 1844 *Manuscripts* and the criticism of Feuerbach in the *German Ideology* and the eleven *Theses*. His criticism of the Young Hegelians is also self-criticism.

He previously spoke of the 'task of history' and of a philosophy 'in the service of history',[12] but now firmly rejects all hypostatization of history. 'History does nothing, it "owns no tremendous wealth", it "fights no battles". Instead it is man, real, living man that does all this, owns and struggles; there is no such thing as "history" that uses man as its means in order to attain its ends – as if it were a separate person – for history is nothing but the activity of man pursuing his ends.'[13]

If the subject of history is stated in terms of such concrete reality, the postulation of a comprehensive metasubject becomes dubious. 'The philosophers have set up as an ideal under the name of "man" those individuals who are no longer subsumed under the division of labour' and have regarded 'the whole . . . process as the process of development "of man", so that "man" was substituted for previous individuals at a different level of history and represented as the driving force of history. Thus the whole process was regarded as a process of self-alienation "of man . . .".'[14] No better treatment is handed out to the idea of 'self-production of the species', in which the 'successive series of individuals connected with each other are regarded as a single individual' who 'carries out the mysterious process of producing himself'.[15]

Marx now consistently directs his criticism at all historical teleology that goes beyond regarding history as the total outcome of the pursuit of individual aims. If 'later history is made the purpose of earlier history' and any 'determination' is imposed upon history as a 'distinctive aim', that is purely and simply a 'speculative distortion'.[16] People should not imagine that it was the plan or intention of previous generations to supply them with material.[17]

At this stage we shall not go into the question of what positive conception of history emerges from these negations, but it can hardly be that which the interpreters of Marxism we quoted above have stated it to be.

B. *History as 'humanization of the ape'*

The idea that there is a normative essence in man that it is the purpose of history to realize having thus been disposed of, the Marxist theory of history as the engendering of true humanity is no longer possible within the conceptual coordinates of Marx's early writings. History is no longer a uniform trend towards the realization of an anthropogenetic programme, but is the, in many respects, 'contingent' result of a highly complex synthesis. The return of the idea of 'humanization' in Marx's and Engels's later writings must be regarded in this light.

Prehistory and human society. In the 1859 preface in which Marx summarizes his theory of society and also discusses 'in broad outline' the course of previous history, the succession of 'economic social formations' (ancient, Asian, feudal and modern bourgeois methods of production), he adds the laconic statement that with the bourgeois, the last socially antagonistic form of economic organization, 'the prehistory of human society' has been concluded.[18]

This is a highly important proposition, but he gives no further information about the criteria by which the future, post-capitalist society is to be established as human society *par excellence*. Does this represent a return to his earlier view of history as the process of realization of man's original nature? The closeness to the formulations of 1844, that postulated a breach between the society that was 'becoming' and society that had 'become', is obvious. But such a return is unlikely, and Marx may have been contrasting socially antagonistic societies with 'human' society. No standards of 'humanity' were necessarily involved; just at the time when Marx was writing this preface he had reaffirmed a conception of human development that lacked any 'previously laid down standard'.[19]

It seems legitimate to assume that the term 'human' applied to post-capitalist society was intended to describe the predominance of universal humanity over social and national particularisms. The elimination of class antagonism would mean that men would no longer face each other as 'class individuals'; in other words, socially divisive factors would no longer prevail over those that united humanity. Perhaps even more important is another idea that Marx closely associated with the prospect of the communist revolution, namely the completion of the process by which history became world history as a result of the coalescence of regional societies into a single, world-embracing society that included the whole of mankind. Only then would there be justification for speaking of human society in the singular. This would give a completely unteleological, pragmatic meaning to Marx's phrase about human society and its 'prehistory', implying the foreseeable and attainable result of a process actually taking place.

Moreover, one thing was clear to Marx from the outset. The society of the future was not its final and immutable form, though some of its foundations would be enduring, i.e., final in that respect. The form that it would assume would be a form of development, and it would thus have a history. It would be a state of affairs in which 'social developments would cease to be political revolutions'.[20]

Final departure from the animal kingdom. When Engels classified humanity in the wider context of the universe, he too delivered himself of a series of propositions on the history of philosophy. Man's role in natural history, he said, had been the development of a new and very remarkable species. The specifically human factor was labour, which in Engels's words had actually created man, and it was characterized both by consciousness and by sociality. This gave Engels something in the nature of a yard-stick by which higher and lower levels of humanity could be measured; the yardstick was the extent to which men consciously planned their activities and cooperated in carrying them out. In his early writings he already made this an anthropological norm, and he stated it as an imperative: 'Produce with consciousness, as human beings, not as separate atoms without consciousness of your species, and you will have elevated yourself above all . . . artificial conflicts.'[21]

The 'struggle for individual existence' that still in many ways opposed men to one another and the resulting course of previous history were an indication that man had not yet completely and finally eliminated himself from the animal kingdom. In his introduction to his *Dialectics of Nature* and in *Anti-Dühring* he said: 'The more men . . . put a distance between themselves and the animal kingdom . . . the more do they consciously make their own history . . . and the more does historical success correspond to the intended goal. But if we apply this yardstick to human history, even to that of the most developed nations of the present day, we find a tremendous discrepancy between the goals aimed at and the results attained, because the basic activity, material production, takes place in anarchy and competition.' 'Darwin did not know what a bitter satire about humanity, and his own countrymen in particular, he was writing when he showed that free competition, the struggle for existence which the economists hold up as the highest achievement of history, was the normal condition of the animal kingdom. Only a conscious organization of social production, in which production and distribution are planned, can lift humanity in the social respect above the rest of the animal kingdom, as production in general has already done for men in certain respects.'[22] Anthropologically the transition to socialism meant that 'the individual struggle for existence ceases. And with this, man for the first time finally emerges in a certain sense from the animal kingdom, leaves behind animal conditions of existence and enters upon truly human conditions. . . . The socialization of men, which previously faced them as a fact imposed by nature and history, will then be achieved by their own free act. . . . Only from then onwards will men themselves make their history with full consciousness. . . . This will be mankind's leap from the realm of necessity into that of freedom'.[23]

There seems to be no essential difference, or at most a terminological one, between this later version of an anthropogenetic philosophy of history and the earlier versions. But perhaps the general formulations do not matter so much as the underlying theoretical foundation, the infrastructure of the concept of history, the analysis of the nature of social-historical developments, the concrete how and why of historical changes. It was to this that the founders of Marxism shifted the emphasis, and they did so to such an extent that they regarded themselves as turning their back on philosophy. That is the implication of the other theoretical approaches to which we shall now turn our attention.

2. HISTORY AS PRACTICE

In Marx's 1844 *Manuscript* the basic theme is not 'history' but a concept of conscious, objective, social human activity that also possesses a historical dimension. His subsequent writings of

1845–6 represent a rectilinear continuation in this respect. He and Engels now direct their attention, not to history as a whole, but to individual situations and actions, to the actors and the circumstances of their action, to 'how' history works rather than to the meaning of history to men.

How history takes place

We have already seen what history is not; it is not an independent agency with its own aims, but the outcome of human actions. 'History is nothing but a succession of generations each of which exploits the material, capital and productive forces taken over from all its predecessors; hence on the one hand it continues the activity handed down to it under quite different conditions and on the other modifies the old circumstances with quite different activity.'[24]

History takes place under definite, empirically demonstrable conditions: the existence of living human individuals with a definite natural endowment in a definite natural environment; and these individuals are productively active in a definite way and accordingly enter into definite social relations. History results from this state of affairs because the production of the means for satisfying human needs does not remain static, as 'the first satisfied need, the action of satisfying it and the instrument for satisfying it that has now been acquired leads to new needs – and this production of new needs was the first historical act'.[25] As men reproduce themselves, the resultant dynamics are such that 'increased needs produce new social relations and increased human numbers produce new needs'.[26]

History is in the first place that of the 'developing productive forces taken over by each new generation and hence the history of the development of the forces of the individuals themselves',[27] or, more specifically, at every stage of history there is 'a material outcome, a sum of productive forces, a historically created relationship to nature and of individuals towards each other', a sum-total of productive forces 'that is transmitted to each generation by its predecessor' and 'on the one hand is modified by the new generation but on the other itself prescribes its own living conditions and imposes on it a definite development, a special character of its own – so that, in other

words, circumstances make men just as men make circumstances'.[28]

As Marx and Engels paraphrase it in the language of archi-
tecture, 'material production' is the 'foundation' of the whole
of the 'real living process' that constitutes man's 'being'. Their
theory of history had to be built on this foundation to include
social totality. The task was 'to develop the real process of
production, starting from the material production of immediate
life, and to interpret the form of traffic connected with and
produced by that system of production, that is to say, bourgeois
society at its various levels, as the foundation of the whole of
history and to portray it in its state action, and explain by it
all the various theoretical products and forms of consciousness,
religion, philosophy, morality, etc., etc., and to deduce the
process by which these things arose from it, after which of
course it will be possible to portray the thing in its totality (and
also the interaction of these various aspects)'.[29]

This states the general position of historical materialism. It
is of course a formula explaining, not so much the sequence
and meaning of social changes, as the definite coordination
between the separate components or 'fields' of social activity;
it is concerned primarily with the static 'working' of a society,
but its importance for understanding changes in social relations
follows. It leads to the methodological directive always to
study 'the "history of humanity" in connection with the
history of industry and exchange'.[30]

Meanwhile historical materialism seems to provide no opening for a 'rational' theory of history. Its attitude is rather completely empirical and actually anti-philosophical. 'With the
representation of reality independent philosophy loses the
medium of its existence. At most its place can be taken by a
summing up of the most general conclusions that can be
deduced from observation of man's historical development.
But unlike philosophy these deductions . . . do not offer any
recipe or pattern by means of which historical periods can be
shaped.'[31] Henceforward in all matters concerning history
Marx and Engels acted as empirical observers. Thus they noted
that in the bourgeois era history had become world history and
that individuals of world-wide historical importance had taken
the place of local ones.[32] Similarly in previous history it was 'an

empirical fact that with the expansion of activity on a world historical scale separate individuals were increasingly enslaved to a power alien to them', but it was 'also an empirical fact that as a result of the overthrow of existing historical conditions by the communist revolution . . . this . . . mysterious power is disintegrated and that thereupon the liberation of every single individual is achieved proportionately to the extent in which history is completely transformed into world history'.[33] Thus communism is represented not as an ideal, a state of affairs that should be brought about, but as an empirical indicative, the *'real* movement that eliminates the present state of affairs'.[34] Marx and Engels make other observations in the same spirit.[35]

On the interpretation of the texts of 1845–6

The passages on the theory of history in the *German Ideology* and the *Holy Family* cannot be said to be especially popular among the interpreters of Marxism. On the contrary, they are rather a nuisance, disturbing their happy preoccupation with the philosophy of history that emerges from the *Manuscript* of 1844. We shall attempt to make plain the theoretical approach that appears in the *Theses on Feuerbach* and the writings of the same period. Some general comments are called for, however. Above all, when Marx and Engels claim to be restricting themselves completely to empirical observation and the welter of conclusions apparently make their premises invisible, this should not be taken too literally. Plenty of problems and theoretical construction in relation to the theory of history lie concealed behind what they say. We must of course always bear in mind the experimental character of the chapter on Feuerbach in the *German Ideology*.

Our question, then, is what understanding of the 'order of the historical process' is to be gained from the writings of 1845–6. As we shall be going into this more thoroughly in later chapters, here we shall mention only the most important points.

1. History is represented, not as a closed process, the rectilinear or dialectical realization of a programme, but as an open process of continuing syntheses in unique situations.

2. Its central theme is not the idea of any process or the form that it takes, but the subjective activity of human beings, their

production, the meaning of their products to them, and the further activities to which these stimulate them.

3. The viewpoint from which the *Theses on Feuerbach* stem is one of practical subjectivity. The accountability of the activities of human subjects, 'individuals', as Marx and Engels repeatedly call them, is concentrated in the idea of the wants and interests transmitted to them in practice by existing subject-object relations as well as men's inter-subjective relations.

4. In these writings the interpretation of the part played by the self in the actual process of world change, in which Marxist theory itself plays a part, leaves a great deal to be desired; it can be asserted that there is here an anti-normative misinterpretation of the self that renders the approach to subjectivism in the *Theses on Feuerbach* ambiguous. We shall see the distortions to which the self-denial of subjectivity can lead when we come to speak of the third of the approaches to a theory of history. One of the starting-points for such aberrations of Marxist theorizing is the narrowly objective viewpoint of the sixth of Marx's *Theses on Feuerbach*.

The concept of 'human nature' in the sixth of Marx's 'Theses on Feuerbach'

Our assertion that the Marx of the *Theses on Feuerbach* assumed a standpoint of practical subjectivity, and that the centre of this subjectivity was human needs may seem disputable in the light of the sixth thesis, which says: 'Feuerbach dissolves religious nature in human nature. But human nature is not an abstraction dwelling within the single individual. Its reality is the sum-total of social relations.' Moreover, Marx says, Feuerbach by his conception of the abstract, isolated human individual had also abstracted him from the 'course of history'.[36] From this it seems to follow that human nature is not to be grasped by retreating into the human 'interior', into the subjectivity of the individual subject.

Marx's sixth thesis on Feuerbach is one of the most important cruxes in the interpretation of Marx's philosophy. A. Schaff rightly points out, however, that, though often quoted, it has seldom been correctly understood.[37] In particular the negative consequences that at various times have been drawn from it seem especially questionable. Thus to J. M. Bochenski it shows that when 'man' is referred to in communist ideology, it is not the individual human being that is meant, but the humanity or society in him, and that it does not recognize the individual as an independent subject at all.[38] Soviet Marxist authors have made extensive use of the Marxist formula and have often regarded the 'sum-total of social relations' as a description not of the 'human *essence*', as Marx does, but of *the* individual human being or personality and this has encouraged the misunderstanding to which Bochenski succumbed. Radical conclusions are also drawn from the sixth thesis by L. Althusser, who regards it as putting in a nutshell a 'total theoretical revolution' that would replace the old paired concepts of 'individual and human essence' with the radically new concepts of 'social formation', 'productive forces', 'superstructure', etc.[39] This leads to a purely 'structural' concept of society, and Althusser finds further evidence for this in the following passage in Marx's 1882 notes on A. Wagner's economic text-book, which he quotes on the fly-leaf of his *Marxisme et humanisme*: 'My analytic method does not proceed from man, but from the economically given social period.'[40] Marx himself explained the methodological reasons for not taking either 'man' or 'men' as the starting-point for his definite analytical purposes.[41] But this cannot possibly mean that a concrete concept of society is possible without the individuals that form society as primary data. K. Korsch rightly draws attention to the inseparability of 'objective' and 'subjective' formulations in Marx's conceptual language. While the former represent history as an objective process in the reciprocal relations of productive forces and of productive relations, the latter call by its true name 'the real historical subject that carries out the objective development in practical action'.[42]

Althusser correctly points out that after the turning-point of 1845 Marx no longer talks of the 'human essence' as a definite pre-existent 'essence', as he did in 1844. But the dropping of this 'idealism' is not, as Althusser believes, the end of what he calls 'subjective empiricism', the view that concrete subjects exist as absolute data. Nor does it mean that henceforward no general concept of the 'human' is possible. Althusser equates the concepts of the (ideally normative) 'human essence' and 'human nature' and dismisses both from the repertoire. He relies on passages written by Marx both before and after 1845 in which he speaks of 'human nature' in an affirmative but certainly not idealistic sense.

But let us now turn to the text of Marx's thesis. 'The human essence', the key sentence states, 'is not an abstraction dwelling within the single individual', but 'the sum-total of human relations'. If one is to understand what this means both positively and negatively, the whole train of thought must be followed very carefully. There is some reason to believe that when he wrote these sentences he was not aiming at a comprehensive statement of an anthropo-sociological position but was setting out to clarify a more particular proposition, namely that the phenomenon of religion (with which the fourth, sixth and seventh theses are concerned) is not to be explained by any general 'human essence', but merely by a historically determined state of society, that the 'religious mentality' is a social product and that the abstract individual whom Feuerbach had in mind belonged to a definite social system.[43]

Marx was here aiming at an anthropological generalization; what he says certainly does not have to be understood as implying a rigorous alternative. In the first place, if the phenomenon of religion is not based on any general 'human essence', it does not necessarily follow that no general human characteristics (or 'nature') exist. Secondly, when Marx criticizes Feuerbach for interpreting 'human nature' only as a genetic characteristic of the single individual, and points out that the essential characteristics of men are intelligible only as the sum-total of their social relations, it does not follow that all that is essentially human is a characteristic only of 'social relations' and that nothing of it appears as a genetic characteristic of the single individual; Marx states specifically that Feuerbach interpreted human nature 'only' as genetic. Thirdly, when Marx further points out that Feuerbach abstracts men from the 'course of history', it does not follow that man is, so to speak, completely absorbed in history and that anthropological constants therefore do not exist.

The 'positive' aspects of Marx's view of man and human nature can perhaps be restated as follows. In practice we always have to do only with human individuals who have in common definite characteristics of the human species (e.g., definite basic wants and the peculiarity of being able to exist only in society). Their social way of life means that some human characteristics are not to be deduced from single individuals but from their form of social organization; further, that some essential human characteristics do not appear in all individuals, but only in some. To the extent that man-made products and productive relations form a part of the 'human essence' and are subject to historical change, 'essence' or human nature is changeable; the 'human nature in general' of which Marx speaks is always moulded and overlaid by a 'historically modified human nature'.[44] To Marx, who regarded man above all as an actively productive being, human nature was a 'sum-total of needs and impulses',[45] a sum-total of behaviour trends.

The concept of 'social relations' succumbs only too easily to a categorical reification. It is nevertheless Marx himself who specifically asserts that all human 'relations' are rooted in the active behaviour of man. 'They begin . . . by eating, drinking, etc., i.e., not by "being" in any relationship, but by behaving actively, actively gaining control of certain things in the outside world, and thus satisfying their needs.' Men are 'continually in active relations with each other and with these things', and among other things they have 'to struggle for these things with others'.[46] That is the concrete meaning that Marx attached to 'social relations'. Where else but in the individual himself is one to look for the ultimate conditions that make these relations possible? (It is also a logical fallacy to regard the human essence or human 'nature' as a mere 'relationship'; relationship or relations necessarily presuppose substantial and active entities capable of having relations in general and relation with each other in particular.)

The *Theses on Feuerbach* are not by themselves sufficient to provide a full survey of Marx's view of 'human nature'. If one takes the other references into account, the following results:

1. When he speaks of a 'universal human nature' he refers to a universal minimum of human characteristics, and not just 'biological' but specifically human, consciously active and socially basic characteristics. These do not consist only of certain basic constants, but are also at work in the general modes of historical modification.

2. When, however, he refers to the human essence as the 'sum-total of social relations' in its 'historical course', he points to a comprehensive maximum and total of essentially possible ways of being and historical modifications of human nature, and to the great multiplicity of what 'man' has already been in the course of history.[47]

3. Finally, between the 'anthropological minimum' and the 'anthropological maximum' there is a level that could be called the anthropological or human 'optimum'; a concept of the 'human' as a norm or postulate (however historically or supra-historically localized). In the 1844 *Manuscripts* Marx quite obviously was speaking of 'human nature' – and its alienation – in this sense; but after his criticism of Feuerbach he retreated from the idea. The idea of a higher level of humanity undoubtedly retained its importance to the 'mature' Marx, but it then had to be based on something other than the idea of an overriding predetermination based on man's true nature.

The change that took place in Marx's thought in 1845 is hardly a total theoretical revolution. Afterwards he spoke, not of the human essence, but of human nature, which he regarded above all empirically as a 'sum-total of needs and impulses', a given but changeable complex of behaviour trends. (A similar attitude is already to be discerned in the *Manuscripts*.) The idea of man's 'being' became problematical to Marx because it was associated with that of a total human 'standard of being' and a supra-historical 'determination'. Henceforward it was dismissed. But the 'idea of succession' of (general and historically modified) 'human nature' also offered a basis for the setting up of standards, so in *Capital* Marx states that in future men should organize their work 'in conditions worthiest of and most adequate to their human nature'. The specific difference between this and the old idea of the normative essence remains to be worked out. But it seems hardly possible to follow E. Fromm, who sees in Marx's concept of human nature an affirmation of the human essence in contrast to the various forms of its historical existence.[48]

3. HISTORY AS A PROCESS SUBJECT TO NATURAL LAWS

Men, Marx says, 'make their own history'.[49] History is nothing but the activity of men pursuing their aims. But on a closer inspection it turns out to be also something else that is not fully explained by men's pursuit of their aims. As Engels more accurately put it, it is the resultant of innumerable individual human actions. True, men make their history by each one of them pursuing his own aims. But, as countless numbers of men are doing this, and as their aims often conflict with those of others, the outcome is generally different from and often actually opposite to that desired. Therefore, as Engels says, so far as the end result is concerned, their conscious motives are of only secondary importance. If this end result, history, is to be understood, one must look for other factors behind these motivations.[50]

Engels begins by pointing out that the 'driving forces' that underlie the motivations of historically active men and constitute the ultimate driving forces of history can be only such as are capable of setting in motion large numbers of men and whole nations, and of lasting action leading to great historical change. So far we are still concerned with the motivations behind human activities. But behind these Engels sees another factor, 'the trace of the laws governing both history as a whole and history in different periods and countries'. Though nothing takes place in the history of society without conscious intention, this does not alter the fact, in Engels's view, 'that the course of history is governed by general laws'.[51]

Here we have the third Marxist approach to a reply to the question of what history is. It is a process of changes in the structure of social relations that takes place in accordance with certain laws. Marx outlined this theoretical approach in the much quoted phrases of his introduction to the *Critique of Political Economy* and supplemented this in later works, in particular in the introduction and epilogue to *Capital*.

The objective logic of social relations

The active agent of history is social man, but the medium or substratum of history does not consist only (perhaps not even primarily) of individual men, but also of what Marx in his first approach to the problem called the 'sum-total of social relations'. In his 1859 introduction he specified the most important constituents of these as the productive forces; productive and property relations, which can act as forms of development of the productive forces or as shackles on them as the case may be; social revolution; the political and legal superstructure; the form of social consciousness; the social being that determines the social consciousness; and methods of production that condition social, political and intellectual life. Thus an abstract concept of society arises as a structural nexus of productions and products. Here we may refer to a note made by Marx in the course of his preliminary work on *Capital*: 'Society does not consist of individuals, but expresses the sum-total of the relations in which the individuals stand to one another.'[52] We have already seen that L. Althusser sees Marx's 'radically new concepts' (the form of society, productive forces, productive relations, superstructure, etc.) as a superior substitute for the old twin concepts of 'individual and human essence'. We take the view, however, that the theorist's task is to avoid all exclusivity and to provide the link between the 'substantial' categories (producers as individuals, tools, products) with the 'dynamic' categories (activities, resultant processes) and the 'structural' and other categories (relations, correspondences, laws, trends). One of the theoretical aberrations in the history of Marxism (connected with a corresponding deformation in practice) is the fact that in the Soviet Stalinist school an 'objective-logical' abstraction of the concept of society has been put in the place of its full concretization.

The principal propositions of historical materialism tell us something about the definite correlation in which the functioning elements of a social system stand to each other. The chief question is how a functional element, i.e., the production of material goods, can provide the 'foundation' for other things (social stratification, political and state organization and power relations, ideals and attitudes, etc.). The theory goes on to say that the dynamic essence of the 'economic foundation' of the social totality is a 'dialectical' relationship between the productive forces and productive relations; the latter always originate as forms of development of the productive forces, but in the course of time come to be shackles on them and are displaced by new ones in a social revolution.[53] This also yields a new definition of history, as the progressive development of the productive forces with periodic changes of productive relation-ships, a series of progressive periods of economic social for-mation.

What is the relationship of all these structures and processes to men and their activities? K. Korsch remarks that the histori-cal development of society as presented in Marx's introduction is predominantly an 'objective process', and that the acting subject of this development is not, or is only marginally, mentioned.[54] True, 'men' enter into productive relations and engage in conflicts, but neither the content nor the modalities of this activity seem to be determined by them; Marx specifically says that the productive relations into which they enter are necessary and inevitable and independent of their will.

The reason for this dissociation is obviously that, though men make their own history, they do not do so in circum-stances they have chosen themselves, but in the circumstances with which they find themselves immediately confronted, or in traditional circumstances; also men are always definitely pre-formed, *are* something definite, and behave in a definite way in accordance with their being. Their subjectively being what they are is thus itself an 'objective' datum always having a definite correlation to the other data of their objective exist-ence. There thus seems to be a firm link between the objective preconditions and the objective results of social action – cer-tainly not over men's heads, but, so to speak, through them. Just as they are themselves the 'product' of the genera-tions that preceded them, so are their actions explicable on the basis of objective conditions. In *Capital* the capitalist is not considered as an individual, but as a personification of economic categories, an agent of definite class relations and interests, a creature of these conditions.

History as a natural process

In the *Manuscripts* of 1844 Marx, still under Feuerbach's spell, saw in history the 'natural history of man'. He subsumed this under a very broad idea of natural history ('the progress of nature to man'), just as he regarded man's unity with nature as a factor in the historical 'realization of being'. Behind this there is obviously a concept of nature closely related to the idea of normative 'being'. Many years later, when in *Capital* he again spoke of social developments as a 'process of natural history', this had a changed, more negative meaning that appears most plainly in Engels's reflection on the naturalness of previous social development and of capitalist development in particular. (The still affirmative concept of 'human nature' does not arise in this context, except again in certain negative aspects, as man's natural reaction to the social conditions confronting him.)

The fact that to Marx development of the economic forms of society is a process of natural history is connected with his belief that under the conditions of capitalist production men do not function as individuals and persons, but as personifications of economic categories, fulfillers of roles laid down by definite class relations and interests. 'My view, according to which the development of the economic formation of society is a process in natural history, can less than any other make the individual responsible for conditions the creature of which he remains socially, however much he may subjectively elevate himself above these.'[55] This represents a continuation of the most general aspect of Marx's early ideas of alienation, which is that the products and relations produced by men become an independent and alien power in relation to their human producers, and that men in the community of their class act only as 'typical' or 'chance', not 'personal individuals'.[56] But the real reason why 'relations' thus establish themselves as an independent entity exercising an alien rule is that men confront each other as aliens. 'Only man himself can be this alien power over men', and it is always 'another, alien, hostile, powerful man who is independent of him'.[57] It was the alieneity to each other of human communities (tribes, etc.) and the alieneity to each other of social classes and individuals within territorial social units that had set the natural course of previous history.

It was Engels who introduced this aspect into Marxism. In an early work of his, the *Outlines of a Critique of National Economy* of 1844, he wrote that the law of competition was 'a purely natural law: not a law of the mind', a 'natural law that depended on the lack of consciousness of those involved'. 'If the producers knew . . . how much consumers needed, they would organize production . . . which would make impossible the ups and downs of competition and its tendency to crisis.' He laid down an imperative to combat this: 'Produce with consciousness, as men, not as fragmented atoms without consciousness of your species, and you will be above all these artificial and untenable contradictions.'[58] In the chapter on Feuerbach in the *German Ideology*, which was drafted by Engels, there is a wider discussion of the idea that hitherto social development 'had taken place like natural growth, that is, not subordinated to a general plan drawn up by individuals who had freely combined'. On the contrary, it proceeded 'from different localities, tribes, nations, branches of labour, etc.', 'each one of which originally developed independently of the others'.[59] Engels continues these reflections in his late philosophical writings. In his 1886 essay on Feuerbach he describes how, in spite of the fact that nothing in it takes place without conscious intention, history, as a result of the reciprocal effects of individual actions that frustrate and conflict with each other, leads to a state of affairs 'completely analogous to that prevailing in unconscious nature'.[60]

All this must be taken into account if the standpoint of Marx's *Critique of Political Economy* is to be properly understood. There is a certain difficulty involved. In the introduction to *Capital* Marx states very laconically that he regards the development of economic forms as a 'process of natural history' that has its 'natural phases of development' and in its movement follows a 'natural law', 'a law of economic movement', the discovery of which was the ultimate purpose of the work.[61] The difficulty is this. Whenever Marx and Engels mention the course of previous history as resembling natural growth, they do so in a definitely critical spirit, implying it to be a state of affairs that must give way to one in which 'men make their history with full consciousness themselves'.[62] Thus the question arises whether Marx really wanted to establish a universal and positive concept of history as a natural process or only to apply the idea to the formation of capitalist society (as the 'economic' society *par excellence*). The latter seems the more probable.[63] But Marx himself encouraged a generalization of the idea of 'a process of natural history' when in his 1873 epilogue he quoted a long passage from his Russian reviewer N. Sieber which, among other things, said: 'Marx regards social movement as a process of natural history governed by laws that are not only independent of men's will, consciousness and intentions, but on the contrary, determine their will, consciousness and intentions.'[64] The 'objective-minded' spokesmen of Soviet Marxist historical materialism eagerly seized on the idea of history as a process analogous to natural history and obedient to natural laws and have systematically developed it.[65]

To Marx and Engels the quality of natural growth hitherto inherent in the social process, and of the capitalist social process in particular, lay above all in the circumstances that men, in what they were and what they did, did not autonomously develop their own potentialities but were subjected or exposed to an external factor, and that they were affected in a manner that was totally external to them by what others, their predecessors or contemporaries, had set in train. Part of the picture was also the fact that most men were and remained mere products of traditional or existing social relations and merely carried out functions characteristic of those relations; their social behaviour followed the pattern of those relations and was, therefore, calculable like a natural physical process. Marx treats the capitalist system as just such a natural mechanism. But he does not regard 'nature' as merely external; as we have seen, he also speaks of the nature of man. Thus there is a certain ambivalence in the idea of history as 'natural history' and the question that arises is what 'naturalness' has to be superseded and what has to be affirmed and established.

The laws of history

Marx comes closest to regarding the social process as a natural mechanism when he speaks of the 'natural laws' of social movement. He says of these laws that they work and establish themselves with 'iron necessity'.[66] 'Even when a society has traced the natural laws that govern its movement', he writes in the introduction to *Capital*, 'it can neither leap over nor decree the abolition of its natural phases of development', but can only 'shorten' and modify the birth pangs.[67] It is in complete harmony with this that there is a necessary sequence of steps in development. 'The industrially more developed country shows the less developed merely the picture of its own future.'[68]

In the epilogue Marx quotes the reviewer who said: 'To Marx only one thing matters, finding the law of the phenomenon in the investigation of which he is engaged', and the quotation ends with the statement that 'the scientific value of such investigation lies in the clarification of the particular laws that govern the origin, existence, development and death of a given social organism and its substitution by another, higher organism. Marx's book in fact has this value'.[69] Thus it seems that in Marx's view of social movement (1) given the initial conditions, and (2) given the ways of behaviour of the elements involved, (3) definite laws will necessarily result in a definite sequence of states of the system, following the pattern familiar to us from Laplace's theory of natural determination.

Did Marx seriously mean this, and did he really want to interpret the whole of human history in this fashion? This is to be doubted. We may conjecture that he was merely paying a verbal tribute to the predominance in contemporary thought of the idea of scientific law. If his work is looked at as a whole and the nature of his statements is analysed, it will be found that everything does not so obviously culminate in the formulation of laws. The talk of laws is often merely an affirmation of the non-arbitrary nature of historical phenomena; sometimes it is merely a figure of speech, indicating that there is some sort of order behind everything. If one looks for laws that are precisely formulated to any extent – i.e., correlative patterns of behaviour of the type 'if A is the case, it follows that B . . .' the yield is not exactly ample; but this does not necessarily diminish the value of the theory. Marx was, in fact, very cautious in making statements about such patterns of behaviour. He was hopeful of being able to do so above all in regard to what he regarded as the relatively 'closed system' of capitalism, and in relation to its economic indices. But this quickly turned out to be very difficult, especially when it came to integrating the behaviour of partial mechanisms into a synthesis of the total development of the capitalist method of production in accordance with fixed laws. His formulations are in fact exceedingly cautious; hardly one of the tendencies demonstrated is not subject to 'countervailing factors' of some sort.

Over and above that, Marx did not attempt to establish a pattern of behaviour based on natural laws for history as a whole. When Engels in his funeral oration credited his friend with the discovery, not only of the law of movement of the capitalist method of production, but also of the 'law of development of human history', it was a rhetorical flourish suitable to the occasion; the 'law of development' he had in mind was merely the fundamental fact of all social life, namely that men must eat, drink, clothe themselves and have somewhere to live before they can engage in politics, science, etc., etc.[70] This has nothing to do with stages of development, and when Marx discusses them, as in his 1859 introduction, he attempts no more than a descriptive outline; he says that ancient, Asian, feudal and modern bourgeois methods of production must in broad outline be regarded as progressive periods of economic social formation. Only the transitions are susceptible to a certain schematization; when higher productive forces have established themselves, new productive relations, state constitutions, etc. follow.

Marx's 'nomological' approach did not get very far, not even as far as has often been assumed from the statements made in the introduction and epilogue to *Capital*. The further the book advances from the detailed and the particular to the synthesis of wider fields, the more does axiomatic deduction from laws retreat behind complex description.

In this preliminary survey we have tried to demonstrate the different approaches to a Marxist concept of history. What we have now to discuss is how they can be combined into a theory of history. At the outset we pointed out the danger of making any one of them in isolation the basis of theoretical construction and thus taking a very partial view of the theory, whether for the purpose of refuting it or applying it to any particular purpose. This danger exists particularly in regard to the more synthetic approaches; that tending to attribute a universal meaning to history, and that leading to an equally universal objective logical ordering of it. In the one case historical materialism easily develops into a historical Messianism, and in the other into a complete mechanistic view of it, and each, perhaps, can be projected on to the other. Hence the many oddities of the 'Marxist' view of history. Here we propose to test the serviceability of the approach from 'practice', the activity of men that produces history. This will not produce handy phrases for review purposes, but has the advantages of greater authenticity. Nowhere – except in instances of applied historical writing that harmonize with them completely – do Marx and Engels speak so specifically and emphatically (and not just incidentally) of history as in their works of 1845–6, in which they state the practical approach. It is at this point that we shall begin our discussion.

Two The Driving Forces of History

Why has man a history? What drives him along the path to changing his way of life, and where does he find the standards for his productions? The Marxist theorists who have tried to build a systematic theory of history on the fragmentary beginnings by Marx and Engels have emphasized different aspects. While some tend to base history on man's inner trends, others try to find an 'objective' base for it in the structural data of the human social way of living. Thus L. Kofler says: 'It is proper for man not merely to aspire to the maintenance of life, like the animals, but to make his disposition to continually higher social and individual development, based on his endowment with consciousness, the driving force of the historical process. Animals only have "development". But man makes "history", in consciousness of himself and with the aspiration to develop all his constitutional potentialities, to "realize himself".'[71] E. Bloch also concentrates on the subjective basis of human activity, the driving force behind the trend to an 'expansion of the self' going beyond mere self-preservation.[72] In the historical materialism of the Soviet Marxist school, however, subjective activity is regarded as the highly conditioned 'product' of material social conditions and as the executive organ of objective laws of social development. The theory of the 'productive forces' of history is here developed completely along the lines of 'objective logic'; history is the result of the dialectics between productive forces and productive relations.

The cardinal problem for a philosophy of history that wishes also to be practical is that of the impulse behind historical change. It is concerned not only with the interpretation of past or contemporary history, but with articulating in practically relevant fashion the self-understanding of those active in making history. We shall first discuss the general Marxist attitude in the matter. In a later chapter we shall discuss its special applications to Marxist history-making, the struggle for communism.

To demonstrate the necessity of a return to 'practice', we shall start from the opposite viewpoint and discuss the attempt to deduce an 'objective logical' view of historical movement.

I. HISTORY AS A DIALECTIC OF PRODUCTIVE FORCES AND PRODUCTIVE RELATIONS

Marx's introduction to the *Critique of Political Economy* yields a formal definition of history that runs on the following lines: History is a sequence of economic social formations resulting from a dialectic of productive forces and productive relations. The dynamic centre of all historical change is the development of the productive forces, to which everything else is functionally subordinate – whether it serves it or takes the form of some other dependent variable. In the historical materialism of the Soviet Marxist school this approach, based on the inherent logic of objective processes, has been systematically developed, as we have said; it is embedded in a system of universal world processes which is held to constitute the materialist dialectics. The latter claim to provide a general answer to the question of the 'driving forces' behind movement and development in the world; the source of all change is the 'contradiction' inherent in all things. The source and driving force of social historical change is accordingly the contradiction between productive forces and productive relations.

The Foundations of Marxist Philosophy[73] explains this as follows: 'The development of the productive forces is influenced by numerous factors: the geographical environment and density of the population, man's growing needs, scientific discoveries, etc. But none of these factors is the basic one, the chief cause of the development of production. The basic condition for the development of production is the productive forces already created by society, and the principal sources of the development of production are to be sought in production itself and not outside it. These sources are the reciprocal dialectical influence of the elements of production, especially the elements of the productive forces, their inner contradictions, and chiefly the interaction between the productive forces and productive relations' (p. 448).

Two inter-connected impulses to movement are mentioned here: (1) those localized in the nexus of the productive forces, and (2) those involved in the relationship between the productive forces and productive relations.

When one looks at the context in which this passage lies, one is struck by the lack of clarity in the concept and localization of the 'driving forces'. First we are told that the 'decisive force' in progressive social development is labour, but elsewhere this 'force' becomes more anonymous – economic development as a whole is stated to be the 'decisive force in all social changes' (pp. 411, 421). In both cases we are told that one process provides the energy for another, but no primary motive force, or even localization of a primary motive force, is indicated that would answer the question of what it is that in the last resort determines the dynamics, the development of society. Other answers given are actually tautological, as when the dynamics of the development of the productive forces are attributed to 'the nature of the process of material production', which is bound to continue because otherwise life could not go on (p. 441). This evades the issue of why and when and in what permanent or special circumstances the circular process of production and the satisfaction of needs turns into the spiral of expanded reproduction. The authors of the textbook in general reject the view that the development of productive forces is the result of the growth of needs; on the contrary, the latter is stated to be determined by the development of production (p. 446). But elsewhere needs come into their own again when the authors state that development can among other things be due to men's desire for an alleviation of the burden of labour and an increase in their means of existence (p. 448).

So far we have been dealing with the dynamics resulting from the interaction between the various elements of the productive forces. Another factor is the 'decisive influence' (p. 448) that productive relations exercise on the rate of growth and the whole nature of the development of the productive forces. We are told that, when productive relations are in harmony with the nature of the productive forces, there is free play for the development of the latter. If they cease to be in harmony with them and hamper their development, they necessarily give way to different productive relations. This is how the 'contradiction' between productive forces and productive relations becomes the source of further development. The Soviet textbook also mentions another factor. A contradiction between productive forces and productive relations must always be resolved, it states, 'because this is a matter of life and death to the development of society' (p. 445). Thus the 'contradiction' becomes a 'driving force' only because behind it there is an agency that requires it; this agency is very summarily described, and actually remains anonymous. In this objective–logical construct the active subjects involved in events are left in the dark. When the question of 'driving forces' is strictly considered, the answer must necessarily involve subjective impulses and active trends and the spontaneity or stimulus from the environment that sets human subjects on the path of expanded reproduction.

Change in the economic base leading to transformation of the superstructure

It cannot be our task here to analyse the Soviet 'historical materialists'' whole concept of society and history – all the ramifications of the complicated system that seeks to describe the relations between the individual functional elements of the 'base' (i.e., the sum-total of economic conditions) and the social, political, juridical and ideological 'superstructures' (the social structure, the state, parties, legal system, political ideas, morality, art, religion, etc.). These 'superstructures' are said to grow out of the base, to be derived from and determined by it, and to be its product and its reflection; they interact with the base and also with each other (pp. 474–5).

A definition of ultimate meaning is of special importance in this context. Behind the various relationships and correspondences (the political system derives from the economic system, and interests, aims and ideas are determined by the economic structure, etc.) a relationship of *service* makes its appearance;

the state, the legal system, morality, religion, etc., invariably serve the interests of social classes (pp. 475–6). It should consequently be possible to arrive at a detailed balance-sheet of social interests and conflicts. The Soviet theorists attempt this to some extent, but no very vivid picture emerges of the interests of consumers, rulers and ruled, etc., and this is notably absent in relation to the question of historical change. Instead they immediately relapse again into restating structural correspondences, such as 'change of the superstructure results from changes in the base' (p. 480), or 'the force that determines the nature of society is . . . not the legal system, but the economic structure, while the law is merely a product, a reflection of the economic structure. This does not mean that law does not exercise an influence on the economic base and does not play an active part in social changes and upheavals' (p. 479).

The situation becomes completely obscure when the authors mishandle an unskilfully formulated paragraph from Lenin's first theoretical work. They say that 'the basic idea of historical materialism in the explanation of the totality of social relations is, according to Lenin, that "social relations are divided into material and ideological. The latter constitute merely a superstructure erected on the former, which develop independently of the will and consciousness of men, as the form (the result) of their activity directed to the maintenance of life." The material are the primary, determining relations, while the ideological reflect the material relations, are derived from them, are relations of the superstructure' (p. 477). In this objective–logical construction the whole – or nearly the whole – of the interest is directed at the connection between one kind of relationship and another kind of relationship, not at the meaning of either to active human subjects. Thus – though it must be admitted to their credit that this is not their last word on the subject – Soviet social scientists have succumbed to that very reification of the concept of relations on which Marx expended his irony; he insisted that the heart of the matter was always the active behaviour of human subjects.

Factors, products and laws

Other positions adopted by Soviet historical materialism show

how far it is possible to be led away from the dynamic centre of historical events by a one-dimensional development of the objective-logical approach, and demonstrate the extent to which this treatment puts pseudo-subjects in the place of really acting individuals. Structural concepts are isolated from their concrete link with human subjects and become 'subjects' and 'factors' of truly marvellous effectiveness, and the human subjects who alone deserve the name of factors are turned into 'products' of the abstractions thus raised to the power of factors. At the same time the constructors of this theory go to work with the excellent intention of not getting carried away in the stream of a factor sociology.

A Soviet social scientist can 'in principle' have no doubt that, as Plekhanov made plain, the only 'factor' is 'social man', and that the only 'forces' in history are the energies with which men pursue their aims and fight out their conflicts. But objective and subjective factors in practice reappear in theoretical work, and not only marginally and innocuously.[74] It is not working human beings that bring to bear their productive and political strength, but 'labour', and, even more vaguely, 'economic development' is stated to be the 'decisive force'. We are not told that producers and managers are faced with professional politicians, legislators and administrators, but that 'the economy' determines 'politics', that the latter has repercussions on the economic base, and that base and superstructure influence each other with unequal determinative force. We are not told that men, who among other things work, consume and quarrel, in the process develop theoretical ideas and make practical plans about the objects in their environment (some of them because that is their profession), but that economic development produces ideas that in turn influence economic development and play an 'active role'. It is not men who behave in this way or that in relation to things and to each other, but relations that behave in this way or that in relation to other relations. Pointing all this out might be dismissed as pedantry. The answer is that an ideological trend is at work when subjectivity is so violently abstracted from itself in the name of an underlying objectivity – to say nothing of the huge waste of scholastic effort applied to turning things into their opposite.

Finally, this play of forces, factors and relations is governed by factors of a special kind, i.e., the objective laws of social life and social development. Again, these laws are not seriously regarded as factors exercising their own effect; on the contrary, they are regarded merely as coordinations between things and phenomena. But because of the great emphasis that is placed on their objectivity they become non-human or anti-human. 'The laws of social development (i.e., not only the laws of non-human natural objects) are objective laws. They are not only independent of men's will and consciousness and activity, but themselves determine men's will, consciousness and activity.'[75] Man's relationship to these laws is one of involuntary or conscious subjection.

This historical process based on objective laws having been constructed, it forms a system of coordinates into which it is by no means easy to fit active human subjects.[76] They are represented as entities that are conditioned in many ways, or often bluntly stated to be products of the objective preconditions of their activity. But when the objective conditions and limitations of their activity – which are of course undeniable – are made predominant and their subjectivity is reduced to a function of those conditions and limitations, conditioning is transformed into reification. As T. W. Adorno has pointed out, subjectivity that denies itself turns into objectivism.[77] What is the corrective to be applied here? It is not, of course, to banish from social theory all the objective factors (that condition human activity), all the non-arbitrary factors in the human disposition and all the structural determining factors in social life. The task is rather: (1) always to relate these factors to active subjects; (2) to grant the subjective a qualitative primacy (for 'objective conditions' are what they are only in relation to definite subjective behaviour trends); and (3) to articulate those aspects of the subject's action that originate in him, are *causa sua*. To perform this task for Marxism one must return to the practical approach of 1845.

We must conclude this critical discourse by pointing out that a return to the problem of subjectivity has now set in in the traditional domain of the objectivist 'historical materialist'. Since the secession of the Yugoslav philosophers of practice, more and more Leninist-Marxist spokesmen have criticized the inadequacy of the position we have described. 'New problems have arisen', W. Maltusch writes in a study of material interest as motivation, 'which can no longer be adequately tackled with the hitherto usual categories of historical materialism, such as social being and consciousness, base and superstructure, productive forces and productive relations, class and class struggle.'[78]

2. SUBJECTIVE DRIVING FORCES

The question of the 'driving forces of history' leads back to another, more rationally phrased question of what it is that motivates men's activities, leads them outside the circle of mere reproduction of their lives to changed forms of production and living conditions. Analysis must be directed to the basic constellation from which such changes arise, and it must be concentrated on the dynamic centre of the process of change, i.e., the human subject, from the viewpoint of his active impulses and his relations both to objects and to other subjects that share in his activity or oppose it. 'The only teleological predicate is the constructive atom of society', as G. Lukács points out.[79] Marx answered the question of 'what is society?' by saying that it was the 'product of men's reciprocal activity'.[80] In view of the acute danger of reification of concepts in social theory, the necessity of continual methodical reference to the activities of the concrete subject cannot be sufficiently emphasized.

It is, therefore, essential to take into account the structure of subjective motivation in so far as it is historically relevant. When Marx speaks of man's 'real nature', he defines it primarily from this point of view as a 'sum-total of needs and impulses'.[81] The fundamental propositions of historical materialism are closely connected with a view of the structure of human motivation.

If Marxist theorists are resolved to appeal less to this inner nature of man than to an objective field that takes precedence over the subjective, there is some reason for it, in that no individual represents an absolute beginning, but always exists and acts as a 'result' or 'product' that is conditioned in many respects. But, if history is to be understood, attention must be paid to the way in which the subject can overstep the limits of his preformation. Thus the question of 'driving forces' presents itself as follows: How do (1) the continued functioning of naturally inherited and historically transmitted impulses, (2) stimuli from the natural and social environment, and (3) spontaneously creative new beginnings combine so as to produce an effect leading to historical change? The first question that must be discussed is the basic stock of natural human impulses that is the agent of all historical initiatives.

We cannot of course attempt here a systematic outline of a theory of historical-practical subjectivity that would be in accordance with Marxism; we shall merely discuss some of the positions that are important in regard to existing interpretations of Marxism.

The system of needs

Marxist theorists have generally been very reserved in their statements about the general nature of human needs, because they have regarded this as an eminently variable historical factor and not as a supra-historical constant. 'In the course of history', E. Bloch writes, 'the so-called "nature of man", so far as the study of the basic human impulse is concerned, has been recast and reconstituted a hundred times . . . there is not even any "natural" instinctual structure to account for hunger. . . . Instead we meet it in the form of a need that has become social and is socially guided, interacting with other social and hence historically variable needs.'[82] There may be justification for this statement in so far as it is a polemical reply to certain obsolete theories, but it is not the whole truth from the point of view of Marxism. The dialectics of change or modification (demonstrated by Kant) should be sufficient to warn us against making false disjunctions, for only something that is 'persistent' can be modified – otherwise the phenomenon is not modification but change. It is above all the constancy of the variable that is evident in this case, and finally Marx himself took this into account in that he assumed a 'human nature in general' behind 'human nature as historically modified in every period', and worked out some of the implications of this idea.[83]

We agree with E. Bloch that Marx's attitude to man was not one of sociological (or historical) relativism, but that he regarded him as an 'identifiable and recognizable being' – though we do not follow Fromm in regarding his 'being' as an ideal norm of the 'truly' human in contrast to his collective historical 'existence'. What needs to be established here is not a human optimum but an anthropological minimum. This can be arrived at by way of a generalization. Though the content of human needs (from food to musical performances) changes in the course of history, change nevertheless takes place within the framework of certain constant types of need that show definite formal structures in themselves and in relation to each other, definite relations of co-variance and modes of modification, and perhaps also typological characteristics. It is these things that, as L. Kofler says, constitute the formal preconditions for human existence in general or, as he specifically says, the 'unchangeable preconditions of human changeability'.[84]

Let us try briefly to summarize the ideas about the nature of basic human needs that are to be found either explicitly or implicitly in Marx.

1. He undoubtedly regards the ultimate aim of human activity as being the preservation of human life. Only in marginal cases is this absolute self-affirmation of life subjected to any limitation or relativization.

The Marxist classics have emphasized in particular one aspect of this self-preservation, i.e., man's ordinary reproduction of himself through his work. The basic insight of historical materialism is 'that men must first eat, drink, have somewhere to live and clothe themselves' before taking cognisance of other things. Preservation of health and defence against dangers to life from the natural and social environment similarly form part of the basic function of the preservation of life. Here the strictest biological imperatives prevail.

O. Šik and other Marxist theorists have independently pointed out that free movement and activity within reasonable limits also form part of basic human needs.[85] All these impulses, together with that of sexuality, can be described as the vital impulses.

2. Apart from the needs arising from sociality as the general condition and form of human life, there are those associated with the specific form taken by socialization in each case. Men make special claims on the social position that they occupy in

relation to other men. The polary structure of the dimension of social demands has been variously described by Marxist anthropologists; K. Kautsky talks of a duality between selfish and social impulses, and L. Kofler of a conflict between I and you relatedness. The point is that human beings in a society have impulses both to act for others and to make claims on others. A primary and general need is to secure the recognition of others, and reciprocal acknowledgement can be of very varying proportions. A limiting case is full equality of acknowledgement based on complete reciprocity (which to Marxism is the anthropological norm for the communist society), while in class societies the opposite anthropological possibility is realized; some demand more acknowledgement from others than they grant in return; they exercise control over the vital energy of the latter, the products of their labour, their fortune in life, and sometimes their life itself.

To Marxism the impulse to social self-assertion or improvement of one's position forms a completely independent dimension of need, irrespective of its entanglement with other dimensions (in particular the social transmission of a share in material possessions). Qualitatively determined social self-assertion can take precedence even over physical self-preservation.[86] Therefore there is justification for talking of specifically social needs.

3. The system of needs includes yet another type of impulse that goes beyond those of vital and social self-preservation and self-assertion; this is the field of 'the development of human forces that is an end in itself',[87] a form of production that takes place in complete freedom from physical needs.[88] Here Marx was thinking primarily of artistic production and appreciation 'in accordance with laws of beauty', of the need for certain 'aesthetic' qualities in the environment, and further of the trend towards disinterested contemplation, of interest in a thing for its own sake and not exclusively because of its utility. It would be wrong to classify these needs as exclusively 'cultural', 'aesthetic', or 'intellectual', for playful physical activity and also activities based on human curiosity must be included with them. A heading to cover them all might be the need for the free play of forces and free self-representation. Marx allotted an important place in his anthropology to the latter when he

said that man produced in 'truly human' fashion only when he did so in complete freedom from physical needs.

Thus the system of human needs is irreducibly multi-dimensional. We have tried here to differentiate between three major aspects of human activity: those of self-preservation, the determination of social position and free, playful self-represent-ation. These components of course never appear in isolation; on the contrary, concrete activities are always multiply cathected. Other attempts at classification have been made in Marxist literature. O. Šik distinguishes between four levels of need: (1) material; (2) motile (work, play, sport); (3) needs arising out of relationships with others (love, community, friendship); (4) cultural (the acquisition of knowledge, art, ideology, health).[89] There is room for criticism here, particularly of the classification of work, knowledge, ideology and health. Even more doubtful is the distinction that is sometimes made between material needs (interests) and ideal needs.[90] It does not seem reasonable to designate 'ideal interests' in the abstract and put them in a separate category. All human activity without exception takes place in the form of conscious activity with an ideational background; similarly all needs (which for their part, after all, are only factors in activity regarded in the abstract) have an ideal aspect. This ideal factor, which is so-called 'consciousness', varies according to the context in which the action takes place. It can be (1) technical reason and ideational productivity in the service of the maintenance of life (the thirst for knowledge can be a component of the need to satisfy hunger); (2) ideal expression of claims for social recog-nition and group interests (ideology); (3) free play in the realm of intellectual production and receptivity.

Now, one of the central problems of Marxism is how the various aspects of human aspiration are associated with each other and how they share in bringing about historical change. The principal propositions of historical materialism are closely connected with a definite view of the structure of human impulses.[91] The proposition that production is the 'foundation' of all social order and that methods of production 'condition' the whole social, political and intellectual life of a society is based on the fact that 'men must first eat, drink, have some-where to live and clothe themselves before they can engage in

politics, science, art, religion, etc.'. That does not of course
mean that politics, religion or art are exclusively a function of
the aspiration for material goods; but it does mean – among
other things – that a considerable part of the energies invested
in political and religious struggles derive from the demand for
material goods.[92] Men call for a new social and political order
because they want to bring about a distribution or production
of material goods that will be more favourable to themselves.
This is of course only a partial factor in the general theory of
historical materialism, just as the Marxist expression 'conditioning' points to a relation of only partial dependence and
not to a total functional relationship. It is not maintained that
political and ideal activities revolve exclusively round questions of production and distribution. The statement that
production is the 'foundation' does not mean that it is the
'means'. Marx regarded as a defect of modern bourgeois society
the fact that in it 'production is the aim of mankind and wealth
the aim of production'. In earlier ages wealth was an end in
itself only to a few trading peoples; normally 'the ancients'
were not concerned with what form of property created the
greatest wealth; the question they asked 'was always what kind
of property created the best citizens'. Thus human wealth, after
the abolition of its 'narrow bourgeois form', was to consist of
nothing but the 'universality of the needs, abilities, pleasures,
productive forces, etc. of individuals'.[93]

It is thus completely in harmony with Marx's outlook that
E. Bloch, considering the priorities of historical materialism
from the viewpoint of the basic human impulses, should
regard the 'primacy of human dignity' as taking precedence
over the 'priority of meeting human material needs'.[94] If there is
such a thing as a 'centre' of the whole complex of human needs,
it consists of the impulses towards the establishment of proper
social position. Marx developed the emotive appeal of personal
autonomy and socialized freedom into a categorical imperative.[95]

The state of development of human needs and their satisfaction

It can be assumed, then, that the fundamental types of human
need form part of the basic human constitution. Their rich
development and the extent to which they achieve or are

denied satisfaction, i.e., the concrete build-up of the system of needs, is part of the historical process. We shall deal with the mode of their historical development in the next chapter; here we shall discuss the Marxist view of the social historical relations between the development of needs and their satisfaction.

In general, needs and the possibilities of satisfying them have undergone an immense expansion in the course of history, though for society as a whole the expansion has been anything but uniform. At all times there have been minorities that have been able without difficulty to satisfy their elementary needs, while in addition laying claim to a whole world of additional material goods, expanding the need for social recognition into the privilege of enjoying special respect and reserving for themselves a wide area for free play activities. Meanwhile large majorities engaged in manual labour have been restricted to an extremely modest amount of development and satisfaction of needs. This historical fact must occupy a central position in any analysis of the dynamics of social behaviour, and on this subject Marxist theory has many contributions to offer. Its central categories are class interests and class conflicts. Its conceptual system of coordinates is defined by the polary types of harmonious-egalitarian and élitarian-antagonistic socialization.

There is a definite connection between the type of human socialization and the social productive forces. What Marxist analysis has to say about the dialectics of harmony and disharmony between productive forces and productive relations is concretely reflected in its statements about the distribution of the burdens and pleasures of life in the light of a definitely measurable total expenditure and yield, dependent on the degree of development of the productive forces, as well as on the proportionate relationship between satisfaction and dissatisfaction associated with the existing method of distribution.

As for the concrete relationship between productive forces and the social order, Marx and Engels developed a historical calculation that runs somewhat as follows. Historical progress means broadly that expenditure of energy on the elementary needs of life tends to decline, thus releasing more energy for the development and satisfaction of higher needs. But this does not take place uniformly, resulting in all members of the society similarly benefiting from the declining expenditure of energy and its growing yield. At the initial low point of labour productivity and the provision of goods, equality in the social distribution of burdens and pleasures to a large extent prevails. But as soon as any considerable surplus over the absolute necessities of life becomes available a minority appropriates it as its privilege, exploits the majority, and rules over it. Modern industry radically alters this situation in that it modifies the division of labour and so increases the volume of goods that social equality at a high level of development and satisfaction of needs becomes possible.

Marxist literature contains many dubious replies to the question why history took place in this way. Most dubious of all is Engels's idea that class privileges had 'a certain historical justification' on the ground that the growth of productive forces and the development of high civilization were possible 'only . . . by means of an increased division of labour'. 'Without slavery in ancient times there would be no modern socialism.'[96] According to this idea, the humiliations of the class society are the necessary price that had to be paid for historical progress – *per aspera ad astra*. But the idea is fallacious and inconsistent with Marxism, and Engels himself put forward considerations that make it superfluous and invalid. The privileged position of some bought at the price of the oppression of others is not a teleological necessity of history but arises as a contingent natural result of existing behaviour trends and practical possibilities – thus as a result, not of the requirements of any historical teleology, but of 'natural causality'. In a basic situation of shortage, men easily find themselves in the position of satisfying the 'need for more' at the cost of others. Also this is not a rational calculation of historical progress; most of the costs are by no means necessary conditions of progress, and most progress would in principle be attainable without them.

Marxist theorists also find themselves faced with another teleological problem. Sometimes the ultimate purpose of productive relations (and of the whole social order) is represented as being a maximal development of the productive forces. The latter are, as it were, the 'subject' of an independent trend of development which productive relations have to satisfy. But that is a crudely fetishist notion that has no place in

Marxism, unless the concept of productive forces is interpreted in a very wide sense, not restricted only to economic productivity. The purpose of productive relations cannot be only to improve the balance of the production of material goods, for man himself is one of the 'productive forces', and not only in his capacity as producer and consumer of material goods. To the producers productive relations are not only the conditions in which such goods are produced, but also constitute in an all-embracing sense the conditions in which they live and work, in relation to which they make multifarious demands, in regard to working hours and conditions, forms of social cooperation and subordination, etc. What matters is not only the gross product, but also the way in which it is brought about and socially distributed.

Certainly there is also the question of how productive relations determine the resultant material production. But there are also other aspects, equally important to Marxist theory and practice, that must be taken into account. In the first place, there is always the practical question of priorities, of which needs are to be met and in what proportion; it will hardly ever be possible simultaneously to provide a maximum of all that is desirable, and in practice a compromise between the different dimensions of need will have to be arrived at. As the young Engels said, the community will have to decide 'to what extent to increase or slacken production, to give in to luxury or restrict it'.[97] Marx was similarly concerned with the question of establishing an optimal relationship between the two 'realms', that of necessity (expenditure on material production) and that of freedom (the development of the forces of play).[98] This question of valuation and apportionment persists right down into detailed planning for work and leisure. The question whether higher productivity can ever do away with the necessity of such compromises remains open.[99]

This problem of the inter-subjective synthesis of the satisfaction of needs is associated with another problem, the inter-subjective balance of distribution of burdens and amenities among the members of the society. Does Marxism provide anything in the nature of an objective yardstick for this? When Engels said that in certain circumstances class privileges had a historical 'justification' (and when Marx pointed out that during the transition period after the downfall of capitalism inequality would be 'inevitable'), it cannot be claimed that there is historical justice in this, or that it is necessary except in the sense of being naturally inevitable; *rebus sic stantibus*, there is merely no one able to prevent it. Those with an interest in doing so simply do not have the capacity or the power. That is the only reason why some men have been able to develop a high culture in which their needs could be developed and satisfied at the expense of others. In this sense the right to social equality or inequality is a question of power. It is one of those situations that (as A. Schmidt has pointedly said) are valid only for so long as men are willing to put up with them.[100]

The needs of the individual in a society (often transformed into group interests) together with the existing practical possibilities always provide a potential of demand and of procuring satisfaction of that demand, and the concrete determination of the latter, with its inner tensions and continual shifts, is a quite central theme of Marxist social analysis. In the last resort men define their needs (and also their claims against others) to the extent that these are awakened in communication with the objective field and roused or repressed in communication between men themselves. The definition of needs (interests) is an objective 'act' *sui generis* in the context of social practice and the making of history. Needs are plastic, and very little is laid down by nature in this field. Also the continually reappearing discrepancies between the arousal of needs and their satisfaction, as well as between satisfaction for some and frustration for others, offer a possible field for practical operations. The current emphasis on the 'socially conditioned nature' of needs conceals the real state of affairs unless it is accompanied by an explanation of how some needs affect the development of needs by others.

In connection with the social balance-sheet in the matter of the satisfaction of needs, one case must be mentioned that was not unknown to the founders of Marxism, though its full significance only came into view later; that is the anthropological possibility of a manipulative, repressive and compensatory diversion of basic impulses in the social field. This represents a problem that has not yet been completely solved by Marxist theory. To Marx religion was the prototype of such surrogate satisfaction of man who either had not yet attained himself or had lost himself again. But the surrogate function of religion, which is predominantly the vehicle of a resigned passivity, is relatively harmless in comparison with imperialist patriotism (as well as anti-Semitism and other anti-attitudes) on a mass scale. We have seen that it is possible to mobilize millions of men against their own needs and the better possibilities of their satisfaction. This makes plain the extent to which even the definition of human needs becomes a central object of strife in an antagonistic society.

3. THE MODE OF HISTORICAL MODIFICATION

Human needs represent a system of inter-subjective dynamic premises to all history, a kind of qualitatively determined human 'self-movement' or spontaneity. Claiming that Marxism seeks to derive all historical activity from the 'conditions of the external world' is striking at the void. G. Del Vecchio is battering at an open door when he points out, ostensibly in criticism of Marx, that the *primum movens* of activity lies in the nature of the acting individual himself.[101] A. Brunner points out that historical materialism cannot explain how conflict can be possible between methods of production and the human situation if man is and does only what is determined by 'social conditions'. 'For human nature has no independence of its own, but is only the result of existing social conditions; thus it would be completely adapted to the latter, and no dissatisfaction could ensue.' [102] This paradox cannot be laid at Marx's door, however. Nowhere does he say that 'methods of production' in the abstract are a *primum movens* as against the productively active man with his wants and needs.

The *primum movens* of history is man, and the question is how action directed to the satisfaction of needs develops into 'expanded reproduction', how modification and expansion of needs take place in the process, and how the human nature that Marx never denies is historically modified. In particular, we are here concerned with whether Marxist theory has anything unequivocal or even ambiguous to say about the mode of this modification. Marx and Engels in fact tried to design a general model. We shall see, however, that history is a very conditioned thing and cannot be derived from any fundamental disposition of human existence.

Models of expanded reproduction

In the *German Ideology* we find an interesting attempt to deduce history from its constant premises. Marx wrote in the margin of the manuscript a sentence that suggests that such constants are the reason why history exists. 'Men have a history', he wrote, 'because they must produce their lives, and they must do so in a definite manner; this is provided by their physical organization, just as it is by their consciousness.'[103] The 'first premise behind all human history is, of course, the existence of living human individuals of a definite physical organization and thus with a given relationship to the rest of nature.'[104] The first 'historical act' in the real sense of the word that is mentioned is the production of the means of the satisfaction of basic human needs, but this turns out to be merely a static event. Not until the next phase do we come to history. 'The second step is that the first satisfied need, the act of satisfying it, and the instrument for satisfying it that has been acquired leads to new needs, and this production of new needs is the first historical act.'[105] On top of that there is human reproduction itself, as well as the circumstance that all this is accompanied by the establishment between men of social relations, which change as developments take place.

This would lead to a very rigid, closed model of the process, a model of production stimulated to expansion by backcoupling to its own products, a kind of 'self-generation of needs'.

But we do not have to wait for later reflections to provide a counterpoint to this; in the *Manuscripts* of 1845–6 Marx wrote a sentence (though he crossed it out again) that excludes any automatism of endogenous progress; he spoke of the external natural conditions of all historical development or nondevelopment.[106] It was clear to Marx and Engels at that time that history was not the result of purely internal impulses arising out of the nature of the human species, was not human 'destiny' arising out of human nature. On the contrary, it took place in an objective and objectively conditioned manner. In

Capital Marx draws attention to the vital part in development or non-development played by the natural environment. A 'too extravagant' nature held man as if in leading strings. 'It does not make his development a natural necessity. . . . It is not the absolute fertility of the soil, but its differentiation, the multiplicity of its natural products, that forms the natural basis of the social division of labour and by the variety of the natural circumstances in which he dwells spurs man on to the diversification of his needs, abilities, means and methods of labour. The necessity of controlling a force of nature, managing with it, appropriating or taming it on a large scale by the work of man's hand, plays the most decisive part in the history of industry.'[107]

Thus the natural external circumstances in which societies lived played an essential part in the dynamics of previous history. Marx also pointed out that the determinative role played by those circumstances was tending to diminish, and that with the capitalist method of production a dynamic system had first arisen that contained within itself the impulse to expanded production. 'Its technical basis is . . . revolutionary, while all earlier methods of production were essentially conservative', he writes in *Capital*.[108] Moreover, the function of the 'geographical situation' has to be considered, not only in regard to natural conditions, but also and even more from the point of view of the social ecology, the topologically transmitted neighbour relations, and the consequent ties and divisions between different territorial units. The critics of 'geographical determinism' have rightly pointed out that the effects on production of natural factors are determined by the nature of the society. It has on occasion been concluded from this that natural factors cannot be historically important unless they have been socially appropriated, i.e., have become elements in the social being. But, as A. Schmidt pointed out in reply to Lukács,[109] to Marx nature is not only a social category, but is also an independent opposite to the social world as well as being its environment. Hence history is not to be regarded exclusively as the inherent and progressive 'logic' of social evolution arising from intra-social driving forces.

In spite of the difficulties to which the attempt to devise a model of expansive development obviously led, Marxist theorists have continually asserted, though with varying degrees of enthusiasm, the immanent necessity of historical progress, in relation to the material productive forces as well as to social practice as a whole. We have already seen that L. Kofler describes the anticipatory function of the human consciousness, the conscious actualization of the possible, as the guarantor of historical dynamics.[110] But 'consciousness' seems here to be elevated in a somewhat 'un-Marxist' fashion to the role of promoter of change. Kofler is entitled to regard the anticipatory function of consciousness as one of the 'formal premises' of new techniques and systems, but not as a dynamic factor tending to change. Awareness of new possibilities alone does not bring about change in the absence of motivation.[111] Man, G. Lukács writes, is a 'creature responding to his environment' and possesses no 'free-ranging consciousness functioning purely from within itself'.[112]

The constant recurrence in Marxism of the idea of the historical process developing from within itself is a legacy from Hegel. M. Merleau-Ponty reduces Hegel and Marx to a common denominator when he writes: 'There is such a thing as a history of mankind because man is a creature who is turned outwards and needs others and nature in order to realize himself, who isolates himself when he takes possession of certain goods and comes into conflict with other men as a result.'[113] In favour of this view is the fact that history must necessarily be regarded as a development of the inherently possible – saying so is actually tautological; there is also the fact that the capitalist method of production really presents itself as a self-producing process, which is why the idea established itself in Marxism. It was no accident that while Marx was working on *Capital* a 'second reception of Hegel' took place in his mind.

In the epilogue to that work he gives a very radical description of the capitalist method of production and, apparently, of history in general, when he says of his dialectics that 'in the positive understanding of the existing they simultaneously include understanding of its negation, its necessary downfall, and see every developed form in the flux of movement, i.e., also its transient side'.[114] But the question arises here of how strictly and universally Marx applies this principle of negation and, above all, how we are to conceive of the more precise articulation of the factors determining such permanent transformation. It is hardly sufficient to regard it as a recognition of the finite nature of all earthly things; Marx must be referring to something more specific. When he says that dialectics are 'by their very nature critical and revolutionary', this does not follow from the general nature of dialectics, but from the analysis of a concrete social situation and the reasons that brought it about. A Marxist theory of social change acquires conviction, not in the abstract, but from concrete application. It is thus inexorably thrown back on empiricism. Thus Marx's statement about dialectics must be regarded as a résumé of his concrete analysis of capitalism. A general dialectics of human-social subject-object relations, or between the creative process and its realizations, could at most be described as a system of coordinates, but not as the origin of impulses leading to change.

If one is to do justice to Marxist thought as a whole, it must be pointed out that it cannot offer a model of purely endogenous anthropo-sociological development that would make it possible to deduce history from a basic constellation of objective social factors in human activity. Expanded reproduction of human life, though an inherent possibility, is at the same time highly contingent. To *homo sapiens* history was not a 'necessity of nature'; at most it was highly probable. It can be represented only by an open model indicating the various possible constellations in which internal (spontaneous) impulses combine with outside stimuli to lead to a productive result.

Spontaneity and stimulus

Thus there seems to be no alternative to opening two accounts, one for the spontaneous impulses and potentialities of human activity and the other for the external stimuli that affect it, and establishing the typical constellations in which they combine to bring about significant changes.

The 'existence of living human individuals', which is the premise of all history, and the specific mode of conscious human activity are sufficient to present us with a tremendous potential, a spontaneous source of effects and productions, the 'driving force' we have referred to under the general heading of 'needs' in the Marxist sense. Now, the impulses to spontaneous activity can, of course, very well result merely in 'simple reproduction'; there is no reason why the basic consti- tution of *homo sapiens* should not have led to a static way of life.

Expanded reproduction is always a response to a specific 'challenge' and, with A. Toynbee, we may distinguish between natural challenges and social challenges. If there is such a thing as a uniform mode of historical modification in the interplay of internal spontaneity and external stimulus, it can be described as follows. The starting-point is a form of 'self-movement' that has become historical; it is questioned or threatened by an external influence, and man's productive 'surplus potential' is revealed in the response-reaction of the existing system, which can cover a wide range, from merely restorative adaptations to bold improvisations. The anticipatory-imaginative factor in consciousness is also revealed here, and above all the 'extrava- gant' nature of human needs. Human productivity always has a 'silent reserve', so to speak, that is activated by special stimuli.

Human wants, whether qualitative or quantitative, are not fixed within narrow limits; no one has demonstrated this more impressively than E. Bloch. The circle of urgent needs and availabilities is surrounded by wishful pictures of richer and more ample satisfaction. Man, says Bloch, is a creature of 'pretty wide impulses'. It is tempting to enlarge the model of the expansion of needs outlined in the *German Ideology* into a universal model of historical development, a model of the productive dialectics between the latent surplus of needs and the latent surplus of ability to meet them existing in the avail- able means of production, actualized in the anticipatory con- sciousness. But Marx's premises suggest the greatest reserve in the matter; we have already noted that he regarded the 'revolu- tionary' aspect of the modern bourgeois world as exceptional. For a surplus of wishes is not necessarily historically produc- tive; it can actually be a passive factor. There also has to be a positive element of determination; if that is present, there is certainly something that can be activated.

The factors that (by way of groups possessing initiative) stimulate societies to new forms of activity and new demands can hardly be reduced to a single denominator. In the early stages of history these were no doubt predominantly the realities and influence of the natural environment; later they increasingly became the reciprocal influences of territorial social units. In addition to that, in antagonistic societies there is also always a considerable amount of internal provocation, particularly in the competitive capitalist system. Finally, in a future society the stimulus to change should no longer be the uncoordinated impact of men on other men; instead the productive clash should be transferred to the minds of cooperating subjects, weighing up their needs in relation to the amenities to which they aspire and the burdens they are willing to undertake in order to acquire them. Only in those conditions will needs become the autonomous regulator of preservation and change. 'The truth of the competition relationship', the young Engels proclaimed, 'is the relationship of the forces of consumption to those of production. In conditions worthy of humanity there would be no other competition than this.'[115]

On the whole it is true to say that men are stimulated much more by other men than by their own products to activities from which change results. The more 'highly developed', socially differentiated social systems always have within themselves, as we have said, a substantial potential of inhibited or diverted instinctual energy, with the result that the question of the origin of the impulses to movement does not arise in such 'primary' fashion. The cause of movements that bring about a radical change in an existing state of affairs is then merely a release of suppressed impulses, and the resultant history is merely a response to previous history in which the repressive conditions arose. Stimuli that have a releasing and liberating effect in this way continually arise in the cyclical fluctuations of the total social (and also international) field of lines of force. The energy of the releasing stimulus can be far smaller than the quantity of energy that has been dammed up. These permanent reserves awaiting mobilization serve as a permanent justification for those initiators who undertake the hazard of trying to bring about radical change and accept the risk of failure.

Thus, if it is true that historical initiatives do not arise out of the spontaneous impulses and potentialities of man's inner nature and the basic modes of human activity, but are always the result of a combination of essentially secondary circumstances and the stimuli resulting from them, it is also true that the stimuli release a much larger amount of spontaneous energy than is included in the quality and quantity of the stimuli themselves. It is this to which justice is not done in Marxist versions of theories of historical change based on equilibrium and adaptation. For all the importance of external stimuli, the vital factor is spontaneous human activity.

Conditioning and conditioned

Marx and Engels, attacking the historical idealism and subjective utopianism of the early socialists, took the occasion to emphasize the non-arbitrary nature of social and historical events, and in particular their connection with material conditions. Lenin was similarly faced with a 'subjective sociology' on the part of the Russian Populists, and in the course of campaigning against them he made a number of pungent statements, such as that an idea is only a definite 'copy of reality' and should be brought back to hard 'facts'.[116] Later he sometimes went even further. 'In his practical activity, man is faced with the objective world, is dependent on it, his activity is determined by it. . . .' he wrote. 'Human aims are in reality produced by the objective world.'[117] In a totally different constellation of circumstances Stalinist social theorists again had reason to proclaim the domination of 'objective conditions' over subjective intentions.

If we are to arrive at a balanced theory in the matter, a critical limitation is required of the claim that the objective side is the determining one, for this can easily lead us to theoretical 'objectivism'. The task is to establish and hold fast to a not excessively 'objective' concept of 'objective preconditions', for a great deal of the latter consists, not of material, objective conditions, but of a definite preformation of human subjects. The 'facts' to which Lenin wanted ultimately to reduce all projection of aims turn out on closer inspection to be human dispositions to act; the real issue was the 'prospect of approval and consequently of realization' of such projection of aims (ideals) 'by the masses'.[118]

Also the objective, material preconditions of human actions in the stricter sense of the word are always what they are only in relation to definite or possible behaviour trends of human subjects. They cannot really 'produce' any definite behaviour, but only 'condition' it, produce real preconditions for it, at a pinch by their presence 'call it forth'. But all active production is activity by human subjects.

These considerations do not diminish the constitutive part played in human activity and history by 'things', both natural and worked up by the hand of man. On the contrary, the task is to integrate them into a concept of objective activity, such as has been impressively postulated by the Soviet Marxist author G. S. Batiščev. It is not men 'and' circumstances that make history, but men that do so 'in definite circumstances'. Strictly speaking, human activity conditions itself; the effect of existing and external conditions is included in human 'acts'.[119] The term 'to condition' indicates only partial, incomplete determination; this should be borne in mind in interpreting the Marxist postulate that methods of production 'condition' the social, political and intellectual life process.

Material conditions certainly impose limitations on action and realization. But the correlation between conditioning and conditioned is generally elastic, as is well expressed by Kant's phrase 'the conditions of the possible'; there is always a larger or smaller degree of elbow-room within the bounds of the possible. Different individuals can use the same circumstances for different ends. Everyone setting about acting historically can and must remind himself that, granted existing material means and existing behaviour trends, there are always in principle possibilities present, either in this direction or in that, other than what is about to happen. Thus, apart from its external (topological) contingency, there is also an 'internal' contingency in history.

Three The Totality of the Historical Process

On the first page of Marx's work there are some exceedingly pregnant phrases that try to answer the question 'what is history?'.

As we have seen, these statements about history as the becoming of total man still to a large extent dominate the philosophical interpretation of Marxism. 'The historical process', Flechtheim writes, 'seems to Marx . . . to be a totality tending towards a goal, combining past and future in a living unity.'[120] According to Adorno, Marx and Engels were never so idealistic as they were in their 'idea of historical totality as one of calculable economic necessity'; Adorno actually attributes a 'deification of history' to the atheist Hegelians Marx and Engels.[121] These generalizations about the overriding aims of history, however, became questionable to Marx himself.

Hence we must discuss in what sense and with what reservations history can be regarded as progress and the development of mankind as 'humanization' from the Marxist viewpoint. The actual significance of a closed, holistic concept of history lies in its inclusion of the future, which it thus makes theoretically available and ideally familiar. In the view of many interpreters, the Messianic aspect of Marxism lies in its substitution for faith in God of something in the nature of faith in history, thus providing a kind of assurance of salvation.

We shall now (1) reconstruct the Marxist idea of history; (2) discuss the problems of its anthropological interpretation; and (3) discuss the way in which the Marxist view of history conceives the future.

I. UNITY OF PROGRESS AND PROGRESS TO UNITY

When Marx and Engels, after their dropping of the 'Feuerbach cult', began discussing history in a more specific sense, they made a definite profession of historical empiricism. Theory, they said, could draw only very general conclusions from the observation of real history and could facilitate the classification of historical material, but provided no 'recipes or formulas by means of which historical periods can be corrected'.[122] Their own contributions to the theoretical reconstruction of history remained fragmentary; there is a yawning gap between their theoretical generalizations about history and detailed examples of concrete historical descriptions. A materialist theory of human history can be extracted from the available fragments only with considerable difficulty. Neither the theory nor its raw material make an impressive whole.

How history takes place

The Marxist conception of history is primarily social and economic; the unit of historical study is the economic social formation of society, a definite social structure based on the state of development of the material productive forces. No less important to Marxism, however, is another dimension of human socialization, the territorial juxtaposition of social units. The two dimensions are combined in Marx's scheme of the sequence of historical periods. 'In broad outline', he says, 'Asian, ancient, feudal and modern bourgeois methods of production can be described as progressive periods of economic social formation.'[123] A striking feature of this is the incompleteness of the list and the lack of uniformity of the classification. Engels came to the rescue by bringing the original 'clan society' into the picture, besides mentioning the slave system as a primary type of class structure in addition to those of capitalism and feudalism. On top of this, of course, there is the anticipation of the classless society of the future. This progression of types of social order is accompanied by a trend towards the integration of dissociated societies (which perhaps developed from a common basic unity) by an intensification of reciprocal relations and the formation of bigger units leading to an all-embracing world society, of which the capitalist world market represented the preliminary stage.

On the whole Marx's pattern is very loose; no strict chronological sequence or continuity of development is indicated, nor is there any suggestion that things must take place 'so and not otherwise'. The reference to a specifically 'Asian' social formation shows how open the scheme basically is. Nor would Marx have been embarrassed if his attention had been drawn to other complications or irregularities, e.g., the not very rare instance of regional societies breaking down. Any narrow schematism applied to the sociological nature of individual social formations would have been just as alien to him. Thus he remarked that Roman society, which depended on slave labour, brought about a development of the exchange of commodities that led to the threshold of modern bourgeois society; and he was also of course familiar with the fact that modern bourgeois society had revived slave labour (in America).

Before Marx comes to speak of different historical periods he outlines a mechanism of social transformation that looks like a universally valid law. He says that productive forces 'develop' and reach a stage in which they are in contradiction with existing productive relations, which then turn out to be shackles on their development and have to be replaced in a social revolution by new ones that can function as forms of development again. This raises the question whether Marx wanted to explain all historical transitions between social formations (in so far as they are genetically connected) by a single law and a similar motivation, and in particular whether he regarded a teleological process as being at work leading to a maximum development of the productive forces, the purpose of social systems being always the fulfilment of that task. Our opinion is that this was not Marx's intention. In describing this pattern of events he was essentially describing the fashion in which bourgeois society broke through the barriers of the feudal class structure and the fashion in which the productive forces of modern industry were going to break through the barriers of capitalist property relations. But he did not feel himself to be under any obligation to explain the transition of the property relations of the society of Roman antiquity to that of medieval feudalism on the same pattern – or to deduce the origin of class society from the 'developmental needs' of the productive forces. The nature of social structures and their modification is thus in every instance unique. The pattern of successive phases drawn up by Marx has only descriptive significance and is not the statement of a rigid law.

The upshot of this historical account of the course of history is a double process of social-structural and territorial differentiation (or dispersion as the case may be) and subsequent reintegration. This process does not take place uniformly or on parallel lines throughout the human *oikumene*, but consists of a long pilgrimage, in which different peoples assume the role of advance-guard at different times and then often fall back to the rear again, while others stagnate at lower or intermediate levels or are drawn into more intensive historical dynamics by the advance-guard. When Marx says in the introduction to *Capital* that the industrially advanced country shows the less developed the picture of its own future, the reference is in reality only to the capitalist period, and then not without reservations, and it does not apply to universal history. He might just as well have said that the more highly developed countries block the way of the less developed to the future of both. History on the grand scale, as is shown by the major shifts of scene, is a highly contingent phenomenon. There can be no question of a parallelism of evolution in all connected and unconnected societies; and a universal connection between them arises only very late, in the capitalist age. Marx noted this in these words: 'World history does not always exist. History as world history is a result.'[124]

History as progress

When he outlined his pattern of the course of history Marx spoke of 'progressive' periods of social formation. But in general he did not pay very much attention to the idea of progress, and was actually sarcastic about it. Hitherto, he said, human progress had borne only too great a resemblance 'to the horrible pagan gods . . . who wanted to drink nectar only from the skulls of the slaughtered'.[125] The statements of idealist philosophers of history about progress to liberty, intellectual autonomy and universal humanity find little support in Marxism, for there is no background force that guarantees them. Marx is closer to Kant's more empirical approach to history than he is to Hegel's view of reason at work in it. Though it occasionally looks as if Marx, like Hegel, regards the generations of the living merely as means in the service of an ultimate end, on closer inspection this impression turns out to be false.

We must first tackle the problem of progress in the terms of Marxist sociology. The structural indices of higher and lower degrees of organization, multiplicity and integration are to be found in them, but these are not sufficient in themselves. To Marxism progress is always the road from lower to higher development and satisfaction of needs. It is considered primarily from two aspects. The first question that is asked is concerned with the relations between man and nature. Has society by increasing its material productive capacity increased its means of existence and security, and, as F. Mehring puts it, achieved 'progress from the domination of man by nature to the domination of nature by man'?[126] The second question is whether this progress of the productive forces is also progress in the quality of social relations, whether it represents an advance from lower to higher forms of human socialization, and how the line of such progress fits in with the actual course of history.

From the Marxist viewpoint the question of social progress is looked at in the light of the alternative possibilities of antagonistic socialization and harmonious, cooperative socialization based on human solidarity. The latter is regarded in principle as the higher. Progress of the productive forces is social progress without reservation if all share equally in the contribution it makes to 'humanity' as a whole; in an antagonistic society it is progress if it brings about an increase in solidarity and cooperation. Thus there are two criteria of progress: whether it increases man's power over nature and diminishes men's power over other men.[127]

If we now join Marx and Engels in looking at the course of history in the light of these criteria, a very confusing picture emerges. The fact that there is no trace of any strict linearity in universal human progress is not the problem. It is justifiable and intelligible that attention should be directed to the great succession of historical formations. But here too an awkward problem arises. Above all, it looks as if the historical phenomenon of the class society makes the idea of social progress radically ambiguous.

In our discussion of the social balance-sheet of the satisfaction of needs we have already mentioned Marx's and Engels's reconstruction of history, according to which progress of the productive forces began by destroying the social equality in the distribution of burdens and amenities that existed originally, progress henceforward being the 'development of a small minority at the expense of the great exploited and oppressed majority'. It was not until modern industry was established that it again became possible that in the future all men might be able to develop their inherent potentialities in complete liberty, and that the development of general wealth might no longer be dependent on the 'surplus labour of the masses', just as the 'development of the universal powers of the human mind' would no longer be dependent on the 'non-labour of the few'.[128]

This inequality of historical progress is made very dramatic in Engels's account of it, because in his writings on early history he paints a very attractive picture of the primitive society that preceded the class society. He seems to establish an empirical basis for the assumption of an original 'non-alienated' way of human life. It was a 'wonderful social system', he says, as it left no room for domination and subjection. An enormous gap separated the 'old free fellow-clansmen' from the proletarians and poor peasants of the present day, to say nothing of slaves. Thus what followed seemed to be a deep degradation, 'a fall from grace from the simple moral height of the old clan society'. But the steep decline into mass slavery, as Engels shows, was the necessary condition for all further historical progress and ultimately for the socialism of the future.

We have already criticized on general anthropological grounds this idea of the inevitable 'price of progress'. At this point some further criticism must be made from the objective historical aspect, using points made by Engels himself in the course of his work. Primitive society was no social idyll, no paradise from which men were driven by the class society; consequently the appearance of class division was not the headlong decline that it seems to be if one merely contrasts the conflicting ideal types of tribal community and class domination. Engels himself points out that for all its magnificence the primitive system had severe limitations, one of which was that the solidarity of the free and equal ended at the tribal borders. In the absence of a specific peace treaty, war prevailed between tribe and tribe; war was conducted with the cruelty that distinguishes men from the other animals, and it often ended, not with the subjection, but with the extermination of a tribe. Thus to the slaves slavery meant progress to the extent that those captured in war were at least kept alive instead of being slaughtered.[129]

This removes a great deal of the problem's sting. The 'dialectics' of human progress no longer 'necessitate' the enslavement of free men so that one day a higher freedom may be obtained; we now see merely that advances in civilization in class society do not benefit everyone alike, and also that it is not only the privileged classes that benefit. If we look at the broad outline of development of social formations, we can discern a progression in the basic and normal forms of social relations and dependences, leading from the compact tribal collectivism and the pitiless warfare of primitive times by way of patriarchal-feudal relations to the modern wage system; and it cannot be claimed that mass slavery was a necessary step in all this; leaving aside the question of big cyclical fluctuations, that appeared principally in times of change, this represents a gain for the working masses. Cruder forms of dependence are succeeded by higher forms.

Closely connected with the advance of the productive forces is a greater differentiation of activities and qualifications, as well as a more personal articulation of the social whole and an increased significance of the individual in view of his functional specialities. What this means in terms of 'human progress', in the sense of protection against arbitrary power, i.e., in terms of the chances of harmonious, egalitarian socialization, can, however, be thought of only in terms of possibilities. Increase in the forces of production also means increase in the forces of destruction. What leads beyond the ambivalence of past progress is effort – concrete and practical effort – to secure man's recognition by man.

The idea of progress in Marxism is essentially forward-looking; existing conditions make it possible to take a historical step forward, to unite humanity into a single harmonious society. Marx felt a practical confidence that has nothing in common with the current 'belief in progress' shared by many contemporaries.

What, then, is the relationship to previous history of the step forward that is now possible and due? To Marx previous history is the basis of future history, above all in the sense that earlier generations accumulated substantial quantities of material goods and knowledge that were passed down to their successors and finally to their heirs of the present day. They did (and enjoyed) all this for themselves, not as a contribution to a great 'historical achievement' to be consummated in our time.[130] To Marx that is the vital, practical link with history. Another positive, though not practical link is the feeling of solidarity with all those who in earlier times fought for a better world, and of pleasure at their victories, small and great. But no theory about the 'totality of the historical process' plays any essential part in the Marxist view of the progress that is possible and necessary here and now. The Marxist view of history is pragmatical, and involves a radical break with all historical metaphysics associated with the idea of history as a whole. In his historical thinking Marx did *not* remain a Hegelian. He says nothing whatever to justify the view that he 'deified' history.

History is based on a totality, the totality of human potentialities. Marxism, behind its view of history as the modification of social systems, has from the outset been concerned with the question of its meaning in relation to the men who make and suffer it.

2. HUMAN BECOMING AND HUMANIZATION

Contrary to the view of many interpreters, the framing of a Marxist formula for the definition of the anthropological content and meaning of history is an exceedingly difficult task. Marx himself began by boldly tackling the problem, but soon beat a sceptical retreat, and later approached it again only with great caution. It is incumbent upon us to maintain a similar

caution. That means that we must not rashly associate ourselves with his early phrases about history as the 'realization of
man's nature' on the way back from his alienated existence.
After the turning-point of 1845-6, Marx and Marxism were no
longer concerned with dogmatically establishing a normative
concept of the essential nature of man. The concept of the
human essence must be interpreted more broadly and more
vaguely, and some well-considered deductions must be made
from such anthropological normativity that still survives within
its borders. The 'original humanity' that survives (and forms the
basis of 'general human nature'), the humanity that developed
successively and disjunctively in history (the sum-total of the
possible historical modifications of human nature), and finally
a form of humanity that at the present stage of history becomes
a political aim and is perhaps capable of maintaining itself
permanently in human society *par excellence* – all these combine
to form a highly complex concept, ranging from the results
of sober theoretical observation to practical affirmation.

Dimensions of human development

When the Marxist view of man is discussed, attention is
generally directed to the desirable characteristics proclaimed by
Marx that amount to an optimum of human potentialities that
it is intended to attain. But this humanist feature of Marxist
anthropology should not be interpreted as committing Marxism to an anthropological norm. E. Bloch rightly points out
that 'to Marxism humanity is a historical goal, not an *a priori*
principle from which conclusions are drawn; it is not a
historical basic certitude, but is non-existent, a utopian premo-
nition'.[131] The 'basis' from which the path of history leads to
'humanity', i.e., 'general human nature', is only in a very vague
way to be regarded as implying an inherent trend leading towards a final goal.

Marx's concept is not that of man who is non-alienated or
has returned from alienation. It is rather that of a specially
organized living creature that has produced a special way of
living and lives in social groups. Some characteristics of man's
activity – his material productivity, his capacity for conscious
reflection and social communicativeness – create the conditions

for a possible history that is capable of realization as a result of various stimuli, and these conditions also represent the possible dimensions of historical growth. The question that arises is what theoretical model enables one to visualize this 'growth' or 'development'.

It was Engels who, long after the naïve idealism of the early years had been dropped, again put forward a positive view of history as a process of 'humanization', which had begun with the original 'humanization of the ape' and was still at work in history. The 'final departure from the animal kingdom' had not yet taken place. Let us see what the dimensions of human existence look like when they are regarded as dimensions of historical development. (1) If the basic characteristic of man lies in the objective productivity of his labour (as Engels says in his work on the humanization of the ape), the whole of the historical progress of the productive forces looks like the logical development of this natural disposition, and the achievement of a surplus of material and materially conditioned cultural goods is its final fulfilment. Engels also works out the historical development of two other basic human characteristics of humanity. (2) If, after the downfall of capitalism, a society comes into existence in which the 'struggle for individual existence' has been superseded on a global scale, that will be the ultimate consequence and final triumph of human sociability (which Engels regards as the opposite of the 'animal' law of the struggle for life). This all-embracing socialization will provide the basis for (3), the attainment by human activity of its high point of consciousness – if men advance to the conscious organization of their (previously anarchical) social production and increasingly 'make their own history with full consciousness themselves'.

The anthropological interpretation of the end-effect of history as the total development of human potentialities can be carried a stage further. E. Bloch sees in man's upright stance (which Engels regarded as a correlate of the use of the hands for work) an alpha leading to an omega – a 'disposition not to bend but stand erect, i.e., a disposition to the realm of freedom' that has increasingly established itself in the history of revolutions. Finally, the triumph of conscious organization proclaimed by Engels can be interpreted as the achievement of a maximum of human protection 'against the impenetrability of destiny'.[132]

Idealism about human nature here seems to be reduced to an entelechy. How can its working be more specifically described? Bloch takes his point of departure from the concept of possibility; man is the real possibility of what has become of him in the course of his history and may yet become in the course of future advances. Possibility includes on the one hand the passive effect of outside circumstances and change in response to them, and on the other the active ability to change. When Bloch sets about more specifically describing these active components, it is no accident that he tends to drop into organic categories, such as predisposition, germ, root, womb, procreation, development, maturation, delivery. Metaphors from practical life also occur; he talks of putting society and nature 'back on their hinges', and of 'things pending in the historical process'. For all Bloch's emphasis on the creative-expansive and open nature of the process, there is clearly a teleological implication. Something essential is still outstanding – classless man, 'the ultimately intended inherent possibility of previous history'.[133]

Attributing such concentration on a single theme to the Marxist view of history and interpreting the historical sum-total of human possibilities on lines so closely analogous to those of the ontogenesis of organisms is open to considerable objections. If organological models are capable of being useful in this context, phylogenesis would seem to be a better source. Like all great innovations in the history of life (adaptation of amphibia to life on land, the development of wings), man's 'biological design' – his upright stance, development of the hand, living in groups – no doubt had a specific 'prospective significance'. But the question is what active function should be attributed to such 'possibilities' and what their concrete effects on the 'development 'of human history are. From the objective balance-sheet of development and non-development we are bound to conclude that the formation of 'orthogenetic series', i.e., the formation of characteristics (such as production, conscious alteration of the environment, degree of social integration), seems from the purely morphological point of view to be a very 'logical' process, but that its real origin lay, not in any inherent law, but in contingent syntheses. Above all, one must guard against granting the separate characteristics that can be enumerated a law of development of their own. The 'development' of human sociality up to the point of the integration of all the members of the species into a single harmonious, cooperative group no more follows a specific law of sociality, or even any law of the basic human constitutions, than ordinary simple conscious, purposeful actions reveal a 'trend' on the part of humanity to become conscious master of the world and its socialization. Such anthropological descriptions are descriptive only. In general it can be assumed that expansive and cumulative changes take place when men within their field of action respond permanently or periodically to challenges by making communal responses. In the Marxist view, the only one of these responses that has had real historical effect is the objectivation of the results of labour in a form that can be handed on. The other effects of 'development' have no independent line. If a closer definition of the putative 'predispositional system' of historical progress is desired, there is nothing to hold on to but the average or exceptional effects of the system of human inherent needs. But, in view of the multidimensionality and wide range of man's instinctual nature, one is on very treacherous ground in trying to pick out constant impulses to a form of progress leading to an increase, not only of material amenities but also of human friendliness, with 'permanent peace' between men as the 'ultimate result'. No doubt there are trends that represent something in the nature of a 'predisposition' to universal human harmony – K. Kautsky describes them in his naturalistic language as the 'social impulses' – but the whole question is how much or how little these impulses have made real history. The progress in the production of material goods cannot be questioned, for all the contingency that has accompanied it. This progress can be regarded as a dimension of the growth of specific characteristics of the human race: the extensiveness and depth of the human impact on the world, the intensity of social interactions, and conscious control of the natural and human world. This in practice means a continuous development of the specifically human way of living and increased human domination over still existing pre-human circumstances. Man is increasingly conditioned, not by nature, but by what he has made himself. In this sense there is justification for talking of an advance in 'humanization' without any teleological implications.

We reach a critical point in pursuing this line of thought when we come to consider the extent to which this increasing humanization of the world of man is also increasing humanization in the vital sense in which 'humanity' is distinguished from the merely 'hominoid'. The two are only too easily confused; often enough the Marxist view of the matter is represented as assuming that humanity – even if it is still outstanding – is implicit in the human way of life (this assumption is always present when anthropological concepts move in the polarity between 'alienation' and the 'true nature of man'). This all too easy assumption must be done away with so that a clearer idea of humanity may be established.

Humanity and history

To the Marxist there is no doubt that egalitarian, harmonious socialization, the opposite of the antagonistic, élitarian type, is the higher and therefore the more 'human'. Its basic principle is equal respect for the 'humanity' in every single individual. In our introductory discussion of the texts we pointed out the undeniable justice with which this concept of unrestricted 'humanity' can claim to be characteristic of the classless and internationally integrated society of the future without thereby becoming involved in any dubious historical teleology; in that society particularisms will have lost practical importance and the only fundamental privilege will be that of universal humanity.

We have already pointed out that, for reasons stated by Bloch, this 'humanity' is not an *a priori* assumption from which conclusions can be drawn, is not axiomatic, but must be regarded conceptually (and in terms of real history) as merely a result that flows from, or more accurately that will flow from, a synthesis subject to many conditions. 'Men, without exception, are not yet themselves', T. W. Adorno writes.[134] It might be possible to deduce the desirable qualities (assumptions, standards, practical principles) of a true humanity from history and genetics, and to demonstrate a process of development of them that must be continued. So far as both ideas and practice are concerned, there is undoubtedly a rich tradition to follow. But does the real history of humanity present us with a picture of progress, however painful and rich in sacrifices? Mentioning the problem of progress in historical and sociological terms itself suggests a negative answer. We believe that Adorno states the true Marxist position when he says: 'No universal history leads from savagery to humanity, but there is a universal history that leads from the sling to the megabomb.'[135] There is no direct link between advances in productivity and advances in humanity, for increased productivity also implies increased destructivity. G. Lukács sees 'inequality of development' in the fact that 'greater humanization of life always produces increased forms of inhumanity' and will do so 'until the process of humanization is complete'.[136] Looked at from the criterion of humanity, the history of man contains a radical dichotomy. On the one hand there have been repeated attempts to develop humanity from the limitations of its elementary forms to greater social breadth which have again and again been cruelly repressed; on the other there is the future possibility of its successful realization, at any rate in broad outline.

Thus from making deductions from history we are thrown back on arguments based on the present and the future. Why does Marxism regard a society of universal peace (denounced by Nietzsche as implying 'the docilization of the democratic herd animal', and in many other phrases as well) as the higher and more desirable? What is the Marxist anthropological norm? There are a whole series of positions in the matter, partly complementary, partly mutually exclusive, that present themselves for discussion and to which we shall return. Our own position is that the future 'human' (i.e., communist) society is a concrete, historically practical project based on real conditions and possibilities. Here we shall merely confine ourselves to some brief comments on the anthropological status of this Marxist 'humanity'. There can clearly only be an 'immanent' basis for this, or more specifically a 'self-legislation' that is not arbitrary but is rooted in the human subject, in his definite self-affirmation. The type of universal socialization aimed at in communism has its instinctual basis in such 'social needs' as the wish for shelter and active solidarity. These enter into a selective synthesis; rivalry impulses will have to be overcome in any case. One characteristic of the Marxist idea of humanity is very important; though 'fraternity' is aimed at, it does not play a predominant part. The strong component in Marxist humanism is not love, but respect, which each individual creates for himself and therefore shows to all others. At any rate for as long as humanity continues to be negatively transmitted by the struggle against the existing contempt of men by men, the necessarily militant demand for respect must remain the principal path to the achievement of humanity. Just as practical subjectivity is the agency of self-legislation for what is to prevail, so is the potential of demand and the ability to put it through as it exists at any one time its own executive agent. On the historical plane it is the organ of 'absolute working out' of new modifications of human nature, with no prescribed yardstick and with the result of previous self-production as its plastic foundation.

If our interpretation of Marxism is correct, the idea of a 'totality of the historical process' loses much of its fascination. History may teach by its examples, but it legitimizes nothing that cannot be legitimized within the field of the present. Perhaps fascination with 'history' is an indicator of present defective practice or, even worse, of lack of present practice.

The search for a brief résumé

If a brief definition of the Marxist view of history is sought for, it should be clear, after all we have said, that finding it is no easy task. It is obviously necessary to avoid the short-cut taken by so many interpreters, who build up suitably selected statements made by Marx and Engels into a theory presenting history as a closed and transparently logical whole tending in rectilinear fashion towards a definite goal. We have tried to throw doubt on such interpretations by reference to the original texts and by putting forward a series of alternative propositions. The view of history that results naturally has the disadvantage of not being summarizable in a striking phrase explaining (except in a very formal sense) what it means in relation to men. We shall, however, briefly recapitulate our amendment of the prevailing 'Hegelianizing' interpretation of the Marxist view of history and its methodical and categorial make-up.

1. History cannot be logically deduced from premises about the human 'essence'. Above all, it is a matter of empirical observation.

2. The reason for this is that history, not only in its secondary details but also its great formations, is highly contingent and not merely the development of an inherent trend.

3. Above all, the circumstance that in 'history' – that complex of connected and unconnected, continuous and discontinuous processes – progress (also describable in anthropological terms) of various elements of human social life and the human relationship to the world has taken place (including among other things, the fact that the complex of parallel 'histories' has begun to integrate into a world history) is subject to this contingency.

4. History is a result, having no inherent 'meaning' of its own, and in particular no meaning in relation to any ultimate goal of its own; it is a dimension of the action of men who reproduce their life and also their socialization in possibly altered form. In considering history, continual reference must be made to the coordinates of motivated action.

5. The contingency of history does not exclude the unfolding in it of a 'law' of human development. But the Marxist 'logic of history' that is so often appealed to is not a rectilinear (even if 'dialectically' contradictory) development towards an ultimate necessary goal, but a disjunctive, multilinear manifestation of a variety of possibilities. Human possibilities include, among other things, definite dimensions for historical growth to which – in contrast to the mere repetition of the similar, such as is represented by the to and fro of territorial possessions – greater interest is justifiably attached.

6. The primary dimension of growth, in which advance over long periods of time and also spreading from one region to another are most readily observable, is the productivity of human labour (with its implications – the multiplication and specialization of activities, the increase in the volume of goods and, to put it somewhat dramatically, human domination over nature); in this field it is easier for progress to be continuous, because there is a greater pressure of needs behind it and the results are most easily accumulated and handed on.

7. Progress in the general quality of human relations is not observable as a matter of historical fact; it can be postulated only in terms of theoretical possibility. If the multidimensional satisfaction of human needs and a wide social distribution of material and other goods is accepted as a higher human objective, the increasing productivity of labour creates in principle the possibility of bringing about, not only a higher degree of saturation with material goods, but also a less repressive and more harmonious form of socialization. The historical result is that men's demand for protection against the arbitrary power of other men tends to be realized on a broader basis. But, because of the multidimensionality of the relations of social forces and the uniqueness of situations of tension, cyclical fluctuations have hitherto been stronger than the long-term trend. Thus history is not progress to higher humanity and freedom, but merely the increased possibility of such progress.

8. The inherent contingency of all history lies in the fact that the realization of the possible is always a matter of free initiatives and creative syntheses, the quality and success of which are not guaranteed in advance.

3. HISTORY AND THE FUTURE

All consideration of history in Marxism is in the last resort an element in practice, looking to the future and directed towards changing the world. As J. Habermas says, it is a 'philosophy of history with pragmatic intentions', and of its relationship to the future he says: 'A historical theory of the existing world adequate to its subject is a theory of changing it'; and Marx said even more positively with regard to history that 'the ability to understand presupposes the wish to act'.[137]

But how Marxism connects history with the future remains a fairly controversial question. Is E. Topitsch correct in saying that Marx seeks 'to gain from the course of history ultimate directives and guarantees for human decisions', that the real 'central dogma of Marxism' is a law of history with 'rational values', and that Marx sets out to establish 'what the next necessary step of world reason will be' in order consciously to take that step, 'thus combining the knowledge of the philosopher and the action of the world historical individual . . . and making himself the irresistible agent of the working of providence'?[138]

Before we discuss how Marxism consciously tries to achieve the future to which it aspires, let us briefly describe its positive and negative, theoretical and practical, attitude to it. In conclusion we shall have something to say about the nature and urgency of the Marxist attitude to the future.

Outlines of the future

The future to which Marxism looks is a society without class differences or nations hostile towards each other, an 'association in which the free development of each is the condition for the free development of all' (the *Communist Manifesto*). From the point of view of the history of ideas, Marxist communism looks like a left-over from the much more detailed and colourful projections and fantasies of the future as developed in the various trends of 'utopian' communism. In comparison, the Marxist view of communism looks distinctly ascetic, e.g., in the *Manifesto*'s concentration on a single point, the abolition of private property. Many polemical passages suggest that Marxism vigorously rejects ideals about a better world; that communism is not an ideal to which reality should be adapted but the 'real movement that is doing away with the present state of affairs'.[139]

By doing violence to these passages, it is possible to arrive at a pure positivism of the 'real movement' (of the revolutionary proletariat) and the pure negativism of its meaning, i.e., doing away with the existing system. Modern discussions of Marxism also occasionally over-emphasize the negativity of the positive or the positivity of the negative, as when Marxists or Marxians of the so-called Frankfurt school reject all suggestions that they should formulate positive ideas about the society of the future and, like H. Marcuse, emphasize the 'power of the negative', consoling themselves with the thought 'that we shall come to the positive soon enough in any event'.[140] Opponents regard this as indicating a grievous error in Marxist theory. E. Kux says that if to Marx the future means, not the realization of an idea, but merely the destruction of a present, it follows that the future to be attained in this way 'is reduced to a present that is always to be destroyed' and the revolution becomes 'a mechanical process to which man is delivered up'. 'Instead of attaining liberty, he becomes the slave of permanent revolution.' Even more drastic is the criticism that Marx does not destroy for the sake of a better state of affairs but 'solely for the sake of (a primarily ideal) destruction'.[141]

Such dramatization of the negativity of Marxism is misplaced; the positive correlate is sufficiently plain and explicit, not only in Marx, but in Marcuse also. The hostility to utopianism of 'scientific' socialism consists solely in the fact that the positive cannot be made concrete to the last degree, but is bound to remain general and theoretical. But, in spite of its generality, it is nevertheless sufficiently concrete to serve, if not as a blueprint, perhaps, at any rate as a compass.

From the scattered remarks on the subject by Marx and Engels it is possible to construct a picture of the future communist society, conveyed partly by positive indications of what it is and partly by negative indications of what it is not. Its most important components are the following: (1) the institutional base is the social ownership of the means of production, which are administered and developed in a planned fashion by the associated producers; (2) the material productive forces are so highly developed that shortage of essentials is eliminated and ample satisfaction of the richly developed wants of all becomes increasingly possible; (3) the more highly developed technology requires and the increased productivity makes possible a general level of education that involves the supersession in the field of production of the 'old division of labour', i.e., the 'great' division of labour between intellectual, creative and managerial activities and repetitive manual tasks; similarly, (4) the factor of domination is eliminated from the administration of communal life and the previous division into rulers and ruled is succeeded by communal self-administration; (5) the broadest distribution of wealth and high cultural development make possible a far-reaching harmonization of human coexistence on a world scale, the end of class conflicts and national wars. Other matters that need concretization are the institutional forms by means of which the collective self-determination of equals can be approached in stages and finally achieved.

Defining the positive aspect of the Marxist projection of

the future raises the question of the degree of perfection, in the sense of definite 'standards of value', that human life and coexistence can and should attain. The vision of the classless society reminds not a few critics of a supernatural vision of paradise, and they classify it accordingly in a category that includes religious ideas in particular, calling it a secularized hope of salvation (which is merely turning upside down the Marxist criticism of religion as an 'apotheosized' and hence alienated aspiration to terrestrial bliss). Thus it is made to look as if Marxist communism aimed at the historical epiphany of the *ens perfectissimum*.

But misplaced dramatization must be rejected here too. There is nothing supernatural about the 'Marxist promise'; it remains completely within finite proportions and limits. There can be no question of eliminating all human suffering from the world. The extent to which the suffering that results from illness and innate physical or mental defects can be eliminated is an open question. How much of the burden of labour, particularly in material production, which to mankind has hitherto been a primary necessity, can be converted into pleasure is a matter about which Marx makes only very reserved predictions. In the field of material production, he says, freedom in the form of self-activation and self-realization is attainable only to a limited extent, for this is a 'realm of necessity', and the true 'realm of freedom', in leisure hours, lies beyond this.[142] So far as inter-human relations are concerned, he makes it clear that, though the society of the future will do away with social antagonisms, that is, those arising from social conditions, it will not do away with all individual antagonisms.[143] Thus the task of communism is to do away with the major evils in the world, but not to bring about the greatest conceivable perfection in all things. It is a step forward, though a very great one, in the finite dimensions of human effort. Hence radically to favour the newness of the new at the expense of all continuity with the past is not really in harmony with the Marxist spirit.[144] The only radically new element in Marxism is its synthesis of indi-vidual elements that were to a large extent present in embryo in the past – just as, according to Marx, reason and freedom have 'always existed', though merely as the privilege of a few.

Communism and personality

Marx's programme of human socialization certainly implies a higher degree of social integration of the individual. As against bourgeois individualism, Marx vigorously emphasizes the social nature of man; man's 'humanity' and his 'social nature' become actually synonymous, for he makes of himself what he makes of himself for the sake of society, and with consciousness of himself as a social being.[145] To contemporary critics of Marx such positions, seen in historical retrospect, through the prism of what was called 'collectivism' under the Stalin régime, look like the point of departure of a process the logical consequence of which is the complete loss of the human personality, its total absorption into the collectivity of the future absolute society. Yet no great effort is needed to deduce from Marx's writings a very balanced view of sociality that, far from extinguishing individuality or personality, gives them greater scope and freedom than they enjoyed under any previous social system. He says that the proletariat must overthrow the existing social system and its state 'in order to achieve the fulfilment of their personality'; an essential characteristic of the new form of 'community' that will take the place of the previous substitute for it is that it makes personal liberty possible.[146] The *Communist Manifesto*, as we have seen, describes the future association between men as one in which the free development of each is the condition for the free development of all.[147] In the first stages of his social anthropological reflections Marx uttered the warning that 'above all it is necessary to prevent "society" from becoming established again as an abstraction against the individual'.[148]

Nevertheless critics have obstinately insisted on finding in Marx the intellectual origins of the odd kind of collectivism that culminated in the human contempt of the Stalinist despotism. The subtlety of the textual exegesis sometimes descends to hair-splitting. G. Dicke reads into the early writings a historical anthropological concept of the coming into being of an absolute identity of community and individual, i.e., an identity no longer coupled with non-identity. This implies the 'absolute society', in which there will be no more reason for the survival of independent individuals. 'Marx himself, and Bolshevism, sacrificed the human personality to absolutized humanity.'[149] G. Brunner tries to corroborate J. M. Bochenski's conclusion from the sixth of the *Theses on Feuerbach* that when communist ideology mentions man it 'does not regard the individual as such' but the humanity in him as the 'concretization of the general', and he produces a quotation from Marx that is intended to demonstrate this. Let us take a closer look at it.[150]

The Marxist degradation of the individual, Brunner says, is plainly shown by the statement that man is 'the totality, the ideal totality, the subjective existence of society as it is inherently thought of'. That is all that he quotes; the context in which these words occur is simply ignored. Let us quote the whole passage: 'Man – notwithstanding the extent to which he is a separate individual, and it is precisely his separateness that makes him an individual and a real individual social being – is just as much the totality, the ideal totality, the subjective existence of society as it is inherently thought and felt to be, as he is also a visible example of the existence of society and its real enjoyment and, as he is in reality, a totality of the expression of human vitality.'[151] One side of a double relationship is thus established in the abstract in relation to the other. Brunner of course overlooks the statement made in the immediate context that 'it is above all necessary to avoid' establishing 'society' as an abstraction over against the individual. But even if this 'other side' of humanity, namely man as a separate individual, is ignored for the moment, it is evident that the statement quoted by Brunner does not mean what he says it does. What did Marx really mean when he said that man as an individual is just as much the totality, the ideal totality, of society as it is thought and felt to be, its inherent, subjective existence? The sentence continues: '. . . as he is in reality a totality of the expression of human vitality'. Thus man as an individual is also in reality *a* (not *the*) totality of the expression of human vitality; and similarly he also exists as an ideal totality of society in the world of thought (the ideal, subjective world as it is thought and felt to be). How then can it be asserted that to Marx 'man' is not an individual but something else? If this 'something else' is a generalization called 'society' or 'humanity', Marx's train of thought brings us straight back to the individual. If this 'something else' is a 'concrete generality', to Marx it can be concretized only in the individual, for the latter is the concrete generality.

G. Dicke does not evade the proposition, to which we have attached so much importance, that 'society' must not be made an abstraction over against the individual, but he interprets it as follows: 'Individual and society are dialectically based, are identical in the light of this explanatory process, and both are only real in that light. . . . Hence identity means at one and the same time the identity of the individual human being with himself and the identity of society with itself. But since that is the absolute identity of both, the distinction between the two can and need no longer be made.'[152] The fact that according to Marx neither can be regarded as an abstraction in relation to the other indeed points to a fundamental identity between them. But the question arises in which direction the false dualism is to be abolished, that of the 'absolute society', or that of the primacy of the individual.

We are faced with a social-ontological problem of categories. Marx stated it as follows: 'What is society, whatever its form may be? It is the product of the reciprocal actions of men.'[153] Society is 'man in his social relations'. Marx said of society, as he did of history, that it was nothing but the way in which individuals existed for each other and behaved in relation to each other. On the basis of these premises the question of the autonomy of being of the individual as against that of society cannot arise. Individuals are identical with society only because society is nothing but the totality of those individuals and the structure of the relations between them; because the concept of society is completely absorbed in that of the individual. It is not by chance that when discussing the foundations of historical materialism Marx and Engels prefer talking of individuals to talking of society.[154]

Thus the categorical dialectic of 'individual' and 'society' loses actuality in relation to the real dialectic of the concrete social inter-personality of individuals and groups; and it is here that the problem of historical change and historical objectives has its place. The practical objective of Marxism is of course to do away with the subordination of individuals (classes) to others, and thus also to do away with the circumstance that 'social' factors (those that are socially binding on the individual) are not universal but particular and are repressive to many individuals, even of the ruling class.[155] The problem of freeing individuals from relations of subordination applies not only to the subordination of individuals to individuals, classes to classes, and nations to empires, but also to the 'social power' of impersonal and uncontrolled 'relations', i.e., those arising from 'blind' social interaction. That is the purpose that Marx and Engels laid down for communism. Its programme was the basis for 'making impossible the existence of everything independent of individuals in so far as it is not a product of previous intercourse between individuals'.[156] The idea that Marx is the destroyer of individual liberty must be planted in one's head very firmly indeed if one is to stick to it in spite of so many statements by him that refute it.[157]

The Marxist projection of the future

In the discussion of the 'essence of Marxism' there is hardly any other point on which controversy rages so fiercely as that of how the communist projection of the future fits into the Marxist interpretation of the world, the individual and history. Before discussing a formula that we believe does justice to the Marxist position we shall deal critically with a number of current interpretations. Above all, we shall deal with some variations of the reificatory notion that Marxism regards the future as predetermined, as man's destiny or, more imperatively, as imposing tasks on man. In contrast to that we shall try to give reasons for regarding the historical actuality of the 'future', not just as something coming to us, but coming to us as the result of practical intentions.

1. *Communism as religious doctrine.* The works of K. Löwith, J. Hommes, R. Tucker and others have caused the view to be widely accepted that Marxism is basically a pseudomorphous religious doctrine of salvation, that historical materialism is really a historical Messianism, that it looks forward to a kind of eschatological redemption, that its attitude to the future is prophetic and that its mentality is that of faith, 'complete'

faith in what it hopes for. 'The whole historical process as represented in the *Communist Manifesto*', Löwith writes, 'reflects the general pattern of the Judaeo-Christian interpretation of history as the working out of a providential plan leading to a meaningful ultimate goal.'[158] 'The dialectical prophet', Topitsch says, 'is not satisfied with making more or less probable predictions based on the sober weighing up of facts . . . but seeks at all costs to attain absolute certainty of the future realization of what he passionately longs for.'[159] Similar ideas abound, such as Topitsch's 'dialectical rhythm, of loss and redemption, or Löwith's 'dialectic of crucifixion and resurrection', or Tucker's 'vision of the world as a battlefield between the forces of good and evil', culminating in Löwith's 'final struggle between Christ and anti-Christ'.

How alien to Marxism such interpretations are has repeatedly been pointed out, e.g., by J. Habermas, who has shown that they constitute merely a dogmatic inversion of Feuerbach's and Marx's criticism of religion. Such interpretations can only be applied to Marx's early writings, in which he still sometimes expresses himself in idealist metaphors, or in occasional rhetorical phrases (as when in an 1856 lecture he described history as the judge and the proletariat as the executioner – a phrase with which Tucker makes a great deal of play).[160] A more general justification for regarding Marxism as a form of religion can at most be found in the continual recurrence of quasi-religious attitudes in the popular consciousness of the socialist movement;[161] but it is precisely these attitudes that are incompatible with Marxist theory.

2. *Communism as a historical goal.* If these interpretations in terms of religion are left aside, it is easy to arrive at a teleological view of history, with communism as its ultimate goal. Marx's early writings provide a certain excuse for this, as we have seen. Marxism, as Topitsch says, then becomes a 'humanist logodicy', the logos of which is a teleological 'law of history' with rational values.[162] We have already quoted Topitsch as saying that Marx tries to establish from the 'course of history' definite directives and guaranties for human action directed towards the future; it is these that are supposed to be deducible from the postulates of Marxism, the purpose of which is to develop from

'the forms of existing reality the true reality that is its ultimate aim'. Topitsch attacks such deduction of what 'should be' from what 'is', with its circular arguments and double concepts of being.

He here continues K. R. Popper's criticism of what he calls the 'historicism' of Marxist theory. Popper regards Marx as a 'prophet of the course of history' (it is this that constitutes 'historicism', in contrast to scientifically useful predictions or predictions useful for the purposes of 'social engineering'. Marxism, he says, is a 'purely historicist theory that sets itself the task of predicting the future course of economic and power-political developments, and in particular the course of revolutions.'[163] This historicism, it is claimed, leads to the stern repression of activism, to the extent 'that we must subject ourselves to the purely irrational forces of history'.[164] This culminates in 'the moral principle of historicism' that 'I see the inevitability of this development . . . hence I make my basic decision in favour of the proletariat and its morality. And this decision is based solely on scientific prediction, scientific-historical prophecy.'[165] The course of history (at any rate in broad outline) is predetermined, and neither goodwill nor reason have the power to alter it. True, the proclamation of the 'impending socialist millennium' had an active meaning to Marx in so far as 'it directed the consciousness of mankind to the impending change and to the roles allotted to them in the play of history'.[166]

Here everything depends on the part played by 'the law of history' as an independent factor in Marxism and on exactly what the celebrated 'law of history' is. Marx vigorously rejected any hypostatized view of 'history'. The course of history provides no directives. No graphs, trends or 'dialectical' formulas about the historical 'process', but only the specific behaviour trends of human subjects specific to the situation can provide the basis for predictions and projections. The real basis for all 'imperatives' lies in such behaviour trends. The predictions made by Marx (whether they turn out to be true or false) are just as far from being a prophetic proclamation of the inevitable as they are from social engineering. If, as Popper suggests, there was ever a struggle in Marx's mind between activism and historicism, the victory would not have gone to historicism. There is simply no room in Marxism for any such metaphysics of the course of history, for history does not have a course,[167] but men make it. It is not history that has an aim, but men who have historical aims.

We have several times mentioned the question of the relationship of Marxism and its projection of the future to a 'law of history', and we shall return to the subject in the next chapter. When Marx and Engels occasionally speak in the singular of a 'law of movement' of the capitalist period or of history as a whole, the phrase is hardly to be taken literally; talking of a single law of history can *a priori* hardly be intended seriously in the theoretical respect. The idea of the whole course of history being governed by a single law is simply inconceivable, and the founders of Marxism never attempted to establish any such law. The 'economic law of movement of modern society' that Marx tried to discover in *Capital* turns out on closer inspection to be an exceedingly wide-ranging and variable complex of structures and functions from which, in a bold theoretical synthesis, he assumed there would result a sufficiently uniform trend of events in a long chain of reactions progressively developing from situation to situation. It therefore seems advisable to revert from rhetoricism about the laws of history to discussion of what Marxism has accomplished in the concrete analysis of historical processes and their structure.

3. *Communism as an implication of the law of historical development.* After what has gone before, it might seem as if we were at last on firm ground in scientifically searching for the touchstone of historical change in the laws that determine the functioning of society. It was this that became the methodological directive of most Marxist theorists. The Marxists of the Soviet school made the discovery of objective laws of historical development the cornerstone of their doctrine, though more in verbal claims than in practical results. Their partisans in other countries, such as M. Cornforth and F. Marek, have also proclaimed the scientific rigour of such laws.

Cornforth claims that it is the task of historical materialism to subject the social processes to rigorous scientific analysis in order to discover their laws and finally to gain an understanding of the laws determining the total process of social development. From the particular laws he deduces an over-riding 'law of progress', a law of adaptation of productive relations to production. 'The working of this law leads in the course of time to the progressive development of human society.' Knowledge of these laws means knowledge of the real forces at work in contemporary society 'and of how this society can and must be changed'. Meanwhile the vital problem is that of the road that leads from theoretical knowledge of these laws to the actual practice of bringing about change. It can hardly be claimed that Cornforth's conclusions provide a satisfactory answer. 'When production overtakes productive relations,' he writes, 'there arises the historical necessity of changing them, so that men may further advance production and enjoy the blessings that this can give them. Bringing about these changes is a historical task. Such a historical necessity and the corresponding historical task are an objective fact, entirely independent of anyone's wishes and intentions.' An example of such an objective fact is that present-day capitalism shows the necessity of advancing to socialism. Making this statement is making a prediction, i.e., that the advance to socialism will probably take place. But more important is the fact that this knowledge enables us 'to regulate our social activity . . . in the light of the discovery of the objective characteristics and laws of nature and society'.[168] F. Marek takes a similar short-cut in deducing the socialist revolution from the 'law of the movement of history'.[169]

There is much to criticize in this argument. We shall discuss later how dubious it is to try to describe all these important matters in terms of laws. The fact that historically relevant social laws are hard to formulate and those that it is possible to formulate are historically not very relevant constitutes a problem in itself. Furthermore, there is the difficulty that scientifically verifiable laws, unlike juridical or moral laws, which set unambiguous standards of the 'thou shalt act thus and not otherwise' type, are correlations of the type 'if x happens the consequence is y'; the consequence holds throughout all variations of the 'if'. In the context of action this yields 'hypothetical' but not categorical imperatives. The necessity of socialism is here the conclusion drawn from a premise that Cornforth leaves unanalysed. What the law means is only that productive relations must be altered to enable men better to enjoy the blessings of production (and perhaps some other things as well). Their wish to do so is assumed. This aspect of the theory seems to need a good deal of amplification. The validation of the necessity of communism still remains dubious. It can restrict itself to a strictly empirical basis, the scientific observation of facts, and on that basis predict the future on the ground that 'men' (a sufficient number of them in a position enabling them to do so) will bring it about. But Cornforth (like many other Marxist theorists) says that such predictions do not constitute the whole of Marxism, for the Marxist theorist with his theory himself shares in the process that he predicts (and not only predicts); he accepts its inherent aim in practice (and perhaps accepted it before he recognized it as part of a process independent of him) and, since he approves of it in practice, it is no longer entirely independent of him.

Thus the consequence is a relationship of practical inter-subjectivity in which Marxist theory is itself a constituent factor; a relationship that can hardly be described in terms of scientific investigation of facts and the establishment of scientific laws. The tools of scientific thought are inadequate to deal with what we have called the primary affirmation of historical progress. What Cornforth says about human intentions in their relationship to objective laws is hopelessly insufficient for the task. 'When we consider the wishes and intentions of men in their social context,' he writes, 'we must ask what influences their intentions and decisions and what determines the outcome of their deliberate actions.' The answer is 'social conditions'.[170] When the thinking observer has realized why so-and-so many workers have become communists, there is still a long way to go before he himself becomes a communist and contributes to as many as possible of his contemporaries becoming communists also.

The question of this extra amount of motivation required was the subject of discussion at an early stage in the history of Marxism when, at about the turn of the century, Kantian and other 'ethical' socialists disputed the adequacy of a purely scientific basis for socialism. With different conceptual co-ordinates, it is still the subject of debate today. Habermas calls it the problem of the 'surplus' of practical theory over pure philosophy (and science); attempts are made to fill the gap with ethical and axiological considerations and ideas based on natural justice.

4. *Communism as a moral requirement based on natural justice.* Communism is not only a prediction; it is also an aim. It is, though Marx and Engels denied it, an ideal, bearing the stamp of humanist values. At the beginning of his career Marx himself declared the communist revolution to be a 'categorical imperative', though later, as a consequence of the efforts to establish the strictly scientific basis of socialism, this idea seems to have been dropped. Some theorists influenced by Kant have sought to revive this principle; following their tradition, they have called it an 'ethical' principle, a principle of what 'should be' not simply to be deduced from what merely 'is'. L. Woltmann stated this position in his account of historical materialism in 1900. In the economic field, he said, socialism meant the socialization of the means of production, but 'in the ethical respect' it meant a social order with equal rights and duties for all. Socialism was 'in the first place an ethical necessity'; its economic programme meant the 'economic fulfilment of a moral law'. The 'feeling of injustice' directed against class society was similarly an 'ethical necessity', and the abolition of class rule was 'a question of ethics'. Those who were to bring this about should, therefore, 'develop ethical strength by means of spiritual and moral education'.[171] Thus, as K. Vorländer says, 'socialism escapes from ethics neither historically nor logically, neither in theory nor in practice', and Marx and Engels, though they tried later to keep this aspect out of their arguments, arrived at their communist views as a result of 'ethical points of view'.[172] M. Rubel has recently devoted a great deal of energy to demonstrating a duality of sociological propositions and ethical postulates in Marxist thought,[173] and P. Bigo extends this to the categories of natural justice.[174] I. Fetscher concludes from the inconsistencies left unresolved by J. Habermas that the practical 'surplus' of Marxist theory over its rationally deducible elements can lead only to an ethical validation of its practical necessity.[175]

'Orthodox' Marxists from K. Kautsky to L. Kofler (and also in an original manner the Kantian M. Adler) have always rejected this 'ethical' supplement to the Marxist programme, though – as L. Goldmann points out in regard to Kautsky – not with complete conviction, or without unintended concessions to their opponents' viewpoint.[176] We should like to add that Kofler's argument fails to be convincing on the central issue because he is one of those who make unintended borrowings from the categories or phraseology of the ethical socialists and adopts a counter-position that is anything but clear (as well as refusing *a priori* to regard the problem as one of philosophical analysis). In his opinion the Marxist view of history as a sequence of higher steps in human freedom and self-realization is a sufficient basis for judging actions to be 'ethical' or 'un-ethical'. 'To the Marxist', he writes, 'it is sufficient to be in possession of insight into the inner forces, trends and directions of the development of history leading to the self-realization of man to be able to make ethical judgements and recognize his own behaviour as being ethically justified. Furthermore, know-ledge of the ethical nature of his aims strengthens him in his power of decision and action; this becomes the source of "ethical responsibility" and driving force in the struggle for a higher social order. . . . It is not sufficient to be only ethical. That is what the leading circles of our opponents often are in a formal sense. To be really ethical one must have historical right on one's side.'[177]

The purpose of resorting to the 'ethical' is often merely the quite general one of showing the relationship of the socialist programme to a system of values or a morality. Here we pro-pose to consider the ethical (or moral) validation of com-munism from a more specific viewpoint, that is, its basis in norms (to use a modern term that is establishing itself in Marxism) essential to inter-personal relations. The fundamental moral norm of which communism can present itself as the historical concretization and universal realization is simply the classical principle formulated by Kant, that men should be regarded, not just as means, but as ends in themselves. In this context L. Nelson has spoken of the 'right' of all rational beings to equal chances of self-determination. This is a moral ideal in a double sense. In the first place, it describes a morally legitimate type of human socialization, and secondly, thanks to its inherent morality as a historical aim, it bestows moral value on action leading towards it. Thus there is both a moral right and a moral duty to struggle for such a social order; those who have claimed this right defend it as a moral duty in the face of others and reply to opponents with moral protest.

We shall restrict ourselves here to discussing the factor of 'moral justification' in the legitimization of communism. The first question that arises is whether there is an independent moral principle that is a premise to all history, and whether it is essential to the 'legitimacy' of communism for it to be based on such a principle. The defenders of the Marxist position have always been concerned to keep what 'should be' distinct from what 'is', though they have often dubiously sought to emphasize their unity, as when Kautsky tries to derive basic ethical principles from the 'observation of reality', or Kofler regards these as included in a 'historical trend', the nature of which he has not subjected to sufficiently radical analysis. It is essential on Marxist principles to do away with the fetishist semblance of a preordained 'moral law' (and of all 'norms of being' in general) and to bring back the constitution of such laws to the field of human activity and to regard them as a form of 'practical action' of a special kind.

The establishment of moral norms takes place in a process of self-legislation that is included in human self-realization. But this self-realization is not (as Kofler argues) a historical trend based on the 'nature' of human 'existence' and underlying human action. Instead it must be regarded as a modification of historically modified human trends and needs. In so far as we are dealing with norms for inter-human relations, we must ask what basic needs and what expansion in the dimension of social needs (made possible by the development of history) tends to the formation of a social order in which human beings cease to be degraded to serve as means for other human beings. The reason why this state of affairs 'should no longer exist' is that men are no longer willing to put up with it. Thus both to Marx and to Kant 'self-legislation' (including moral self-legislation) is a matter of the 'will', of the practical aspiration of human subjects, not determined either historically or un-historically.

What is shown by the empirical observation of reality (on which Kautsky relies) is that men in society make demands on each other and are ready to grant each other things going beyond concrete exchange relations; that is, mutual respect and aid. A definite amount of this is always required by the social code, and underlying the codification is the potential of demand and ability to put through the demand reached at that particular stage of history. Unfulfilled moral demand becomes the starting-point for a new codification. One of a number of factors in the socialist attack on the private ownership of the means of production is the codification of a specific moral demand, that in the future it shall no longer be possible for anyone to exploit others through his possession of capital.

All this may seem too empirical and descriptive and thus hardly suited to be a basis for the establishment of norms. The validation of moral norms, that is, of what men are permitted or forbidden to do in relation to others, becomes no more than a subjective validation ('making them valid') and no sort of objective yardstick. Certainly one must go beyond the mere objective observation of facts. The only question is where. Is anything gained, either theoretically or practically, by basing norms on some 'objective' factor over and above human inter-subjectivity? The Marxist answer must be that what matters is the practical actuality of the 'validation' in all its weight and significance, which means regarding it, not only as a matter for empirical observation, but also as a challenge to practical action. There can be no 'deeper' validation of norms than that which lies in the inter-subjective synthesis of the self-affirming being of subjects from whom they originated and to whom they apply. All the 'objective' validations that can be suggested, whether a divine will or an inherently valid law of nature, turn out to be merely pseudonymous duplications of an original affirmation in the subject who is his own justification.

Also it will not do to judge the moral 'correctness' of action in a fashion analogous to that in which one judges the correctness of propositions, i.e., by a formal lack of contradiction of the will (i.e., it loses its rights if it wills something that cannot be willed by all). This merely conceals the material premises. It does not logically follow from the relationship of the individual to the general will that there should be one law for all; there is nothing illogical in claiming privilege for one's own will. The criterion of applicability to all becomes normative only if all men have previously been recognized as of equal worth, in a spontaneous act. Hence in relation to communism 'moral justification' does not mean that the latter is deducible from any absolute overriding moral law, but only that a moral factor is an element in the case for it. A premise-and-conclusion relationship between communism and any 'moral principle' exists neither in one direction nor the other. The principle that men shall cease in future to use each other as objects of exploitation does not follow from any overriding principle of justice, but is equivalent to saying that they (beginning with those most concerned) are no longer willing to tolerate exploitation. The 'unconditioned' validity of a principle of this kind means merely the refusal of those committed to it to accept any circumstances whatever as justification or excuse for exceptions to it. Thus there is no argument against those who reject 'the life of the herd' in the name of an aristocratic or heroic ideal of life, but only a practical veto. On the other hand, communism itself is not an overriding principle from which moral legitimacy can be exclusively deduced.

A lack of clarity on this last point arose in Leninism-Marxism because Lenin in his speech to communist youth in 1920 expressed himself very vigorously to the effect that communist morality was completely subordinated to the interests of the proletarian class struggle. 'We say', he declared, 'that morality is what serves to destroy the old exploiting society and to unite all the working people round the proletariat which is building up a new, communist society.'[178] Such statements should not be over-exposed to theoretical interpretation, but another sentence should be noted that the critics tend to overlook, namely that 'morality exists to elevate human society and liberate it from the exploitation of labour'.[178]

5. *Communism as the highest good.* Thus it turns out that communism involves moral principles, but that these are integrated into a further complex of postulates; or, to put it differently, communism is a system of values and therefore itself a supreme value. Some of its contemporary spokesmen have declared it to be such a supreme value – the form of social order in which the whole of humanity is assured of the greatest possible degree of happiness.[179] This claim is based on a theory of

values in human life and civilization. The appeal to 'values' has become popular in wide circles, and in the Marxist camp Soviet philosophers, with characteristic scholastic methodicalness, have systematically set about working out a Marxist axiology. Men, by reason of standards of value and the emotional acts of acceptance or rejection underlying them, become conscious of what the objects in their environment mean to them (not only of what these things are 'in themselves'). Values are a factor in men's practical relationship to the world. Their subjective correlate is that men in accordance with their needs at any particular time want certain things and seek to avoid others. An exceedingly high value is attached to communism by thousands of millions of men because it provides for all the ample satisfaction of richly developed material, social and cultural needs; or, in axiological terms, because it provides an abundance of vital social and spiritual-cultural values. It is not only objectively necessary as a natural historical development, but is also desirable.[180]

Attempting to establish a Marxist axiology invites criticism on principle. This is directed above all at the dualist separation of fact and value, reality and the ideal, judgement of being and judgement of value, and also at certain dubieties in the categories of value (their relapse into pre-scientific forms of consciousness and the formation of fetishist and reifying concepts). As L. Goldmann has shown in his criticism of M. Rubel, P. Bigo and others, the dualism of the ethical-axiological approach betrays a deficiency in dialectics that has already been spoiled by the structure of western languages; an empirical and rationalist culture that is many centuries old has established a radical distinction between the cognitive, affective and active modes and created no terms to describe the totality of human relations to the world.[181] Thus in the interpretation of Marxism there developed a polarization into a value-free scientism on the one hand and a moralism that makes judgements of value on the other. Goldmann does not reject out of hand all justification for differentiating between judgement of being and judgement of value, but he takes the view that these are factors that have, so to speak, been 'done away with' in Marxist analysis, for judgement of value in Marx is never independent of analysis of reality and is therefore not 'ethical', while judgement of being is not objective and value-free and is thus not 'sociological'; understanding, explanation and value are inseparably connected in the dialectical analysis.[182] Goldmann thus attacks the moralizing interpretation of Marxism and normative interpretation of it in general. 'Marx's criticism of economic and social reality', he writes, 'is not intended to be moral criticism that judges that reality in the light of eternal human values or any kind of normative idea; it is intended only . . . to express in the field of scientific thought a criticism that is contained as a potentiality, a really existing force, in the reality that is being examined and is already preparing the way to the supersession of that reality.'[183] The arguments of Soviet Marxist critics of Soviet axiology tend in the same direction.[184]

Working with predicates of value in Marxism is subject to important reservations, but not to a total ban. Dialectics cannot dispense with them completely, but can only 'dialectically cancel out' the categorical dualities in a process of continual reintegration of what has been conceptually analysed. So far as value relationships are concerned, this reintegration can be carried out without great difficulty if the analysis is thorough enough; one has only to show clearly those elements in 'reality' that are the 'potential', the 'really existing forces' that are working towards its supersession. (This cannot of course be done in terms of 'reality' and 'values' – therein lies the limitation of purely axiological categories.) The Marxist theorist does not apprehend 'values' with a view to applying them to social reality, but as a living individual feels unsatisfied needs and joins others who feel similarly. 'Values' cannot be hypostasized or put on a strictly 'objective' plane. A thing has value only in relation to an active subject, and it is on this subjective factor that any Marxist axiological analysis must concentrate. In this context predicates of value are only correlates of objective practice. Communism can no more be based on the ideal validity of a system of values than on a 'moral law'; the most that is possible is an axiological transcription of the desiderata of which it is the synthesis.

6. *Communism as object of hope.* The Marxist anticipation of the future has an interpreter of quite unusual originality in E. Bloch, who has actually made the philosophical investigation

of the future his lifework. He regards Marxism as the philosophy of the future, as tomorrow's conscience, as 'informed thought directed to changing the world'. 'The light in the glow of which the whole uncompleted process is reflected and advanced' is, in his opinion, hope. He calls hope the 'positive affect of expectation', but in his thinking passive expectation of the future increasingly yields to positive activity; hope is confidence, short of certitude, that active realization will achieve its purpose. Nevertheless the element of passivity remains fairly strong in him. This is shown by his description of historical progress as a dovetailing of 'subjective' and 'objective factors' and his attribution to the objective factors of something in the nature of a 'trend' inherent in a 'process'.

His attempt to interpret this process as a kind of 'history of being' of matter has exposed him to the criticism that he is 'ontologizing', and thus depriving philosophy of its practical and critical potency, for historically active men would be working as the agents of something else, that is to say, of matter.[185] To us this criticism does not seem entirely justified. For the 'matter' of Bloch's world process is essentially not something other than man, but his substratum, our very own *materia ultima*. True, his relationship to the *materia prima* seems dubious when he declares that matter needs its boldest form of organization, the Promethean man, 'actively to set the tracks in the right direction for the healthy workings of the process'.[186] This anthropomorphous relationship can be criticized, but nevertheless it imposes no duty on man, it is not a system in which man has to look to something other than himself for directives and standards for his actions. Thus the language of historical materialism that is used turns out to be no more than a meta-categorical transcription, not an appeal to an ultimate outside authority.

Nevertheless the criticism of what in some quarters nowadays is called (not very happily, in our opinion) 'ontologizing', by which being or happening that is not activity within the power of the subject is chiefly meant, is not completely misplaced in Bloch's case. Under the heading of 'objective factors of the economic material trend' he establishes something on the soil of history (not referring primarily to the matter of the world) that stands in contrast to the subject, and in this dualism of object and subject there is no room for the concept of practical inter-subjectivity. What does making historical decisions 'at peace with the process', or 'in alliance with the objective factors of the economic material trend' mean?[187] What does the statement mean that in Marxism ideals are not established by theoretical abstraction, but are set by the 'trend' and are to be developed 'out of history'?[188] Is the historical process here established as an independent entity, an outside power exercizing legislative authority over the subject, something 'other' in fact? But that 'other' can only be others, that is, other subjects, and in principle they cannot enjoy higher legislative authority than I myself. Bloch's theories not infrequently encourage misunderstandings, as when he says that Marxism has discovered in the social being of the proletariat the process the real dialectics of which have only to be made conscious for the theory and practice of the revolutionary ideal to be revealed.[189]

But Bloch is not the philosopher of an objectivity to which the subject is subordinated. On the contrary, in his basic ideas he describes subjective modes more clearly than they are described elsewhere in the Marxist tradition. What he does not offer is a theory of inter-subjectivity, of the social synthesis of objectives and the practice that brings them about. Also a great deal of what constitutes the real work of 'real transition' to communism is missing. 'The real transition', he says in the introduction to his *Prinzip Hoffnung*, 'recognizes and activates the dialectical trend implicit in and taking place in history.'[190] What he says about 'being at peace with the process' is especially revealing; one should be at peace with the process so that 'death statistics themselves brush against the grain'. But what is there to indicate the process that indubitably possesses this quality and invites to peace instead of to dispute? It can hardly be denied that Bloch's ideas betray something of the practical position in which he found himself in relation to 'the process' of the Stalinist régime. He associated himself with an inadequate practice, hoping that it was or would become adequate. Hope as the chief description of a philosophy of the future and of world change based on Marx here reveals a deficiency that marks it off from complete theory-cum-practice.

7. *Communism as practical project.* After all the things we have said it is not, how are we to define the positive meaning of the Marxist attitude to the future? Our answer is an entirely unsensational one; communism is a practical project, localized in concrete historical conditions, that differs only in its dimensions from the projects that men, whether individually or in groups, conceive and carry out in the ordinary course of life. The project of a classless social order is negatively motivated by the many privations suffered by a significant proportion of members of society under the capitalist method of production (and other things associated with it), and by the 'natural foundation' of a historically developed structure of trends and needs of human groups that have reached a definite level of demand. Positively, the communist projection of the future is motivated by the means at the disposal of modern industry which actually or prospectively imply the end of those privations.

The key practical problem of communism is to develop from the group particularity of its origins to taking effect on a general social scale. For this a general consensus is required, and to bring this about there must be a practice that must include various components, of which the first is the determination of the communists themselves. This is not based primarily on a scientific prediction. It is not as if Marx first scientifically 'discovered' the historical role of the proletariat and then adapted himself to that insight. But communists gain courage and confidence for their work from scientific analysis of and prediction based on what is taking place independently of them, and of the calculable or probable behaviour of those who for the time being are 'the others'; that is, the behaviour of capitalists to each other and in relation to the workers, their reactions and their tendencies to react. (The communist analysis is certainly not disinterested, but is uninfluenced by interest.) Determined action by Marxists must be integrated into scientific calculation, with the result that it ceases to be mere scientific calculation, but becomes calculation with a scientific base.

Thus the Marxist's purpose depends on actualizing existing and potential trends. In view of the arbitrary behaviour of the utopian socialists, this aspect of the matter was so important to Marx and Engels that they modestly allowed the postulatory aspect of their programmatic ideal to take second place behind the 'real process'.[191] But there can be no real doubt that, for all its anchorage in material conditions, Marxist calculation of the future is an affirmation of needs and claims. Marxist socialists in their practice are concerned with equating the level of demand of others to their own and awakening in them the same readiness to act, at first for the revolutionary struggle against the existing state of affairs and then for the construction of the new social order. If another description of this approach to the future is wanted, it can be called a 'pragmatological' or – in terms of its aims – a 'eudaemonological' one.

Popper asked whether the Marxist attitude to the future is one of historicist prophecy or 'social engineering'. It is neither. We have already dismissed the notion of prophecy, but something remains to be said on the difference between social engineering and what Marx calls 'revolutionary practice' and is described as an identity between the process of changing conditions and human activity or self-change.[192] Genuine revolutionary practice is not social engineering in which society is divided into two, into operators and objects of their operations, into educators and pupils. The object of revolutionary practice is to lead men away from all situations in which they are mere objects; this takes place in its highest form in the inter-human communication that the Czechoslovak Marxist philosopher M. Machoveč has called 'dialogue'.[193] Social engineering can be only a marginal phenomenon, chiefly when Marxists assume a government function.

The certainty that the 'advent' of communism enjoys in Marxist thought will again engage our attention in the concluding chapter on historical determination. If communism is regarded purely pragmatologically, there can be no ultimate guarantee of its historical triumph. The only question is of the success of a difficult enterprise that depends on many factors, in the assessment of which many unknowns have to be taken into account. There is no law of nature that guarantees the success of the higher objective. As we saw in connection with Bloch's concept of hope, Marxist 'faith' in the future is confidence, falling short of certainty, that the project will be successful – perhaps with qualifications. Though the alternative 'socialism or barbarism' does not, as R. Luxemburg erroneously believed, come from Marx, the idea is nevertheless completely in his spirit. The chances of success of the historical enterprise of communism are included within the 'natural' premises of human social behaviour but, though they are scientifically assessable, they can never be without risk. Marxist politics has always been conscious of this, and it is not the task of the Marxist philosophy of history to compensate for this by theoretical blustering.

4. FUTURE AND PRESENT

The fact that Marxism presents itself as a philosophy of the future has exposed it to the suspicion that it makes the present secondary to the future, sacrifices the happiness of the living to the future paradise of the classless society. L. Landgrebe claims that Marxism turns the self-producing human race into an absolute, and makes the process of that production the only thing that takes place for its own sake. He says that the individual is called on to sacrifice himself to that process, that 'the individual as such has a right to his own existence only to the extent that he serves the attainment of that aim'.[194] But that is not the Marxist position. History is not a process in which the individual stages and actors are subordinated to an ultimate purpose as if they were mere means to an end. One should not be led astray on this point by Engels's apologia for slavery.

Discussion of the costs and sacrifices involved in historical progress only too easily goes badly astray. One mistake consists in discussing the question in insufficiently concrete terms, neglecting the careful examination of responsibilities. K. Rahner cannot be completely exonerated of having fallen into this trap when, as against the Marxists, he holds up Christianity as a protection against the temptation of 'pursuing justified worldly aspirations with such violence that each generation is brutally sacrificed to the next, the future thus becoming a Moloch, to which real man is sacrificed for something that is always outstanding and is never achieved'.[195] The Italian Marxist C. Luporini has stated that this is always an acute danger to communists, and that caution is therefore required in deciding how much jeopardizing of men's personal claims is acceptable as the price to be paid for the future of humanity.[196] But the real Marxist problem should here first be disentangled from other considerations.

What are the costs and sacrifices of historical progress? W. Benjamin has said that the historical materialist cannot contemplate without horror the origin of the goods and documents of civilization, because they are all also documents of barbarism.[197] The Russian post-Hegelian V. G. Belinsky called on Hegel (whose categories, so far as the philosophy of history is concerned, provide more excuse for this than do those of Marx) to take account of all the 'victims of history'. It must be pointed out, however, that only very few of them were really victims of *progress*. But to the extent that they were such, the calculation often goes astray in another respect. Not only do conservative apologists make great play with the cost in lives and suffering involved in the revolutions of the oppressed, while accepting as normal the far higher human costs of the wars of the ruling class, but it is a highly questionable procedure to set the costs exclusively against the gains made possible by them. This results in totally false comparisons, as between human life and cultural achievements or improvements in the standard of living, or reflections on whether the end justifies the means. To Marxists the question has never been whether the human costs are justifiable in relation to the end aspired to, but rather whether the sacrifices of the revolutionary struggle and subsequent reconstruction are not less than those involved in the continuation of the *status quo*. It should be obvious that the total of the human costs of change should not be charged to those who bring it about. The question that must always be asked is that of the costs arising from resistance to those changes.

Within the limits thus prescribed, the Marxist revolutionary is faced with the problem of what contribution he can make to minimizing the human cost of the struggle. There is no doubt about the principle that the human costs must be kept to a minimum (and not on 'one's own side' only). Mysticism about 'sacrifices for the cause' is alien to Marxism. Above all, it must be made plain that the cause for which sacrifices may be necessary is not an abstract future or an ideal future humanity.

If sacrifices for the sake of the 'future' are involved, they are sacrifices for the sake of the future of concrete men. Moreover, the future with which we are really concerned is not so far ahead as all that; the men in question are already living, and any sacrifice of life would be for their survivors and immediate descendants, not looking beyond their grandchildren. The more immediate Marxist problem is to make sure that a revolutionary leadership does not rashly shoulder responsibility for unnecessary sacrifices.

Four Historical Necessity

Since time out of mind there has been a great pother about the determinism involved in the Marxist theory of history. There are in fact innumerable references in Marxist writings to the necessity or inevitability of the historical outcome, not only of single events, but also of developments covering whole periods. Only a small further step needs to be taken to make the whole of human history seem to be a strictly determined process governed by inexorable laws. Marx never specifically takes this step, but there are a number of pointers in that direction, in particular the comment of a Russian reviewer quoted in the epilogue to *Capital*. This states that Marx regarded social movement as a natural historical process governed by laws that determined the human will. This was the origin of the 'Marx of the law of history', the prophet of its ineluctable course.[198] We still have not seen the end of the ancient dispute started by R. Stammler, who pointed out that believing in historical necessity and at the same time calling for revolutionary action was as senseless as founding a party to bring about an eclipse of the moon.

The special characteristic of Marxist determinism is that it declares a basic process, that of economic development, to be the ultimate determining factor in the complex totality of the movement of history, as Marx announced in his 1859 introduction. This has led to the view that economic determinism is a better description of the Marxist theory of history than historical materialism.[199] Economic determinism seems to give a specially irresistible quality to the predetermination of history. T. W. Adorno writes: 'The claim is that the primacy of economics leads with historical stringency to the happy ending inherent in it; that the economic process produces political systems of government and transforms them until they necessarily bring about liberation from economic compulsion.'[200]

The object of the whole of our previous discussion has been to make the point that reifying concepts should be eliminated from the discussion of Marxism. In our discussion of the objective-logical approach we saw that such categorical fetishisms are concentrated above all in the field of historical determination; they dissolve as soon as the pragmatological meaning of the Marxist categories is regained and law-governed events are seen as motivated and conditioned. In this chapter we shall draw attention to some further considerations that assist in the demolition of fetishism about law and necessity in the interpretation of Marx.

1. SOME NOTES ON 'ECONOMIC DETERMINISM'

In the introduction to the *Critique of Political Economy* we are not yet directly faced with the problems of historical determination. The subject is the qualitative correspondence between the associated 'aspects' or 'spheres' of social life that are then, of course, shown to play their part in all historical progress. The points successively made by Marx are as follows: (1) Depending on the stage of development reached by their material productive forces, men enter into definite productive relations that are necessary and are independent of their will; (2) productive relations (or the economic structure of society) are the basis, the superstructure of which is the state and the legal system, and definite forms of social consciousness correspond to these; changes in the latter are based on changes in the economic base; (3) the material methods of production condition the social, political and intellectual life process of the society; (4) social being determines social consciousness, and not *vice versa*.

A great deal of interpretation and dispute has centred on these propositions, and not without good cause. We most definitely do not share the view of G. Del Vecchio, who sees no occasion for misunderstandings here, and says that this clear text should not be obscured by commentaries.[201] Here we shall inquire only what kind of determinism and how much of it is involved, and how complete and thorough is the determination of the social whole by its economic base that Marx claims.

In these propositions he does not speak of one kind of correlation only, but of several: that between social being and social consciousness is not the same as that between basis and superstructure. He uses different terms in each case; 'correspond', 'condition' and 'determine' have different determinative meaning and force. The strongest term, 'determine', is applied to the correlation between being and consciousness, but the determining agent, 'being', is essentially heterogeneous and in a way indefinite. Social being is not merely the method of production, but includes the political system, family relations and all practical activities. What Marx is saying is that the significance of the acts and contents of consciousness lies in the context of practice. For the more specific determination that proceeds from economic factors he uses the comparatively weaker term 'condition'. Basically this means merely that certain assumptions underlying political and intellectual and cultural activities and attitudes are included in the sphere of economic production. This does not amount to a claim to a total one-way determination. The same applies to the third term used, 'correspond'. All explanatory passages and descriptions of social conditions confirm that economic (or technological) determination of the social, political and intellectual life-processes of society is in the Marxist view incomplete and leaves plenty of elbow-room for concrete variations.

The relationship between the sphere of economic production and all the rest is not to be understood as a causal relationship, and in particular not as one of total production. Politics, religion, art, etc., are not the results of the production of material goods; all that Marx claims here is that changes that take place in them correspond to changes in the sphere of production. When Adorno says that in Marx economics take precedence over politics, which are merely a derivative of economics,[202] that is not an accurate description of the Marxist position. It is not claimed that economic changes always come first in time and that other changes follow; simultaneity is also possible. At first sight the relationship can be described as one of functional dependence, but little is gained by that. More accurately it is a 'basis' relationship; one thing is the 'basis' of the other. But this too remains an external characteristic unless the concrete determinative link and the localization of that link is borne in mind. For this, however, it is necessary to go back behind the 'objective-logical' determination of social spheres and activities, processes of change and relationships of dependence, to the 'logos' of the living activity of socially linked individuals. Behind the order of 'basis' and other relations there lies the order of urgency of activities in the human context; 'basis' relations and their correlatives are such in the realm of human ends and means. For social 'relations' are constellations of human behaviour. The 'economic determination' that comes into play must be described in terms of the motivated and conditioned behaviour of living men. Marx's and Engels's statements of the general position of historical materialism make this plain; men must in the first place see to their food, clothing and shelter before they can concern themselves with other things. That of course implies no primacy of value for material goods, but merely a primacy of being or conditioning; it does not even mean a permanent predominance of 'material' needs over others, for when material needs have been satisfied they lose their actuality.

In the Marxist view economic determination in the positive sense of the term consists above all of a double relationship of dependence. In the first place, many social, political and cultural achievements depend on a 'corresponding' degree of material productivity having been reached; an example of this is the great assessment of historical progress made by Marxism. The 'economic factor' does not supply the motivation, but is the indispensable means for the production of something that may be desirable on other grounds. This kind of economic determination – the determinative significance of the material productive forces – will always remain. Secondly, and different in nature, there is what can be described as the economic motivation of extra-economic activities, systems and organizations, that is, social stratifications, political institutions, formations and actions, and finally artistic, religious, philosophical and other productions and ideas. The Marxist position is that economic interests are always involved in these things, though not economic interests only. Real economic interest in the acquisition of material goods and amenities cannot of course be strictly separated from the interests of the ruling group. But we do not believe that Marxism must necessarily cling to the one-sided view that rule is exercised solely for the purpose of acquiring goods or depends exclusively on material possession. In this area it seems more appropriate to think in 'social economic' rather than in purely 'economic' terms. The fundamental Marxist propositions about politics and ideology are in fact less concerned with showing that a special economic interest is the motivating factor in every case than in quite generally demonstrating the class interests rooted in productive relations. The fact that special economic motivations can be demonstrated often enough in concrete instances, e.g., the medieval crusades, is not the central point.

The idea of economic interest also appears in an 'objective' guise, particularly in Soviet Marxist literature in the form of economic necessity, objective economic requirements, and particularly the need for the development of the productive forces. Thus it is stated in the *Foundations of Marxist Philosophy* that until recently the abolition of class differences was 'in contradiction to the requirements of economic progress', but is now an 'objective necessity' corresponding to the 'needs' of that progress.[203] There are at least three objections to this view of 'economic necessity': (1) The reification involved in the elevation into an 'objective need' of the interest of social groups; (2) the misdescription by which the 'negative economics'[204] that justifies class privilege ultimately becomes a positive vehicle of progress; and (3) the too narrow concentration on the 'economic'. (The necessity of historical progress is multidimensional; the desire for more material goods is only one highly important factor in it.)

The predominance of economic motivation will not last for ever. On the contrary, it will progressively decline as further technical progress and the rational organization of society lead to the production and distribution of goods ceasing to be a problem. Thus the component of 'economic determinism' is a historically conditioned and temporary phenomenon. As A. Schmidt has said, the much reviled economic determinism of the materialist theory of history will apply only for so long as men are willing to tolerate it.[205] The only qualification that this statement requires is that the other kind of economic determinism, which to Marxism is the primary one, so far from being similarly abolished, will survive intact; for the retreat of the determinism of economic motivation is itself economically determined, in the sense that it is economically conditioned.[206]

All this can hardly be summed up in a few brief phrases, as T. W. Adorno tries to do when he says of Marxism that the primacy of economics will lead with historical stringency to the happy ending inherent in it; that the economic process produces political conditions which it transforms until the inevitable liberation from economic compulsion takes place. Economic determinism is here developed into an 'idea of historical totality as one of calculable economic necessity'.[207] In defence of Marxism it must be pointed out that it does not put forward the 'primacy of economics' as a universal principle or claim the existence of such things as a 'universal economic process' existing as a historical meta-subject with its own inherent trends. The appropriate category of historical calculation is not that of any central, monothematic necessity, but of possibility. The 'economy', or more specifically the development of the productive forces, creates conditions that make certain things possible. Whether the opportunity of achieving human emancipation (including liberation from economic compulsion) is used depends, not only on the economic process and the conditions arising from it, but also on the impulses of active human subjects. Here lie the limitations of any theory of merely economic determinism.

2. CAUSALITY AND LAW IN HISTORY

However much or little historical determinism exists in Marxism, the most general concept contained in it, not restricted merely to the economic field, is that of necessity. It is anything but an elementary concept; on the contrary, it is a highly synthetic one which we shall leave to the final stages of our discussion. In the Soviet school, where determination has been most consistently developed, we are presented with laws, and in particular laws of social development, as the real structural factor in historical determination; determinism here is determinism based on laws, and the problems it raises will concern us later. This caused the idea that everything in history is the necessary result of causes, i.e., the historical causality type of determinism, to retreat somewhat into the background, though no one would dispute the validity, relevance and stringency of causal determination in the social field. Let us go briefly into the matter.

Historical causality

Among Marxist theorists it is chiefly Max Adler who has allocated a prominent place to the principle of causality. To him Marxism means the 'consummation of the theory of causality', since it includes social action in modern study of the subject.[208] 'Causal observation' is here regarded as the basic characteristic of modern scientific thinking.[209] In history we are of course faced with a special human (psychical) or social causality that differs from inorganic or organic causality, but is nevertheless characterized by the same strict ineluctability.[210] The specific feature of social causality is that the 'objective aspect of events' is combined with an aspect of subjective experience'. The form of consciousness in which it plays its part is that of the will, and it is related to aims and associated with values and ideals, 'as a result of which the whole relationship of human action to aims, values and ideals becomes an immanent element in the psychical causal context'. But from the aspect of objective happening this whole process of willing is subject to the same causal necessity, in particular in relation to those parts of it that stretch into the future.[211] The task of social science is to expand the knowledge gained from 'comparing the results of the analysis of complex social happenings in individual causal series into as great as possible an understanding of the whole'.[212]

Such statements make it necessary to consider the place that can be rightly claimed for causality in the Marxist interpretation of history. Causality is generally defined as the determination of a later event by an earlier one. Looking at it cursorily, it means that the later event is a necessary product of the earlier, but closer analysis shows that determination is in fact a highly complex matter. Causation in the narrower sense means that a movement of an object produces definite corresponding changes in another object. But the nature of these changes is determined not only (and often not even primarily) by the actual action of the cause but also and even more by the nature and state of the object affected. The impact is combined with the mode of self-movement taking place at the time in the object, the determinative part of which cannot be described in terms of causal relationship.[213] So far as the external causal impact is concerned, a multiplicity of factors of very different importance are always involved. This means that in relation to human action cursory observation of causality has little cognitive value, for the inner situation and movement of a purposefully acting subject is more important than the external impact. There is also another factor. Causal determination is rightly held to be dynamic. But as soon as one sets about determining the qualitative (and quantitative) correspondence between the preceding and resulting movements and their effects a categorial problem arises. On the one hand it seems appropriate to bring correspondences that can be described as general within the category of laws; in so far as we are dealing, as in this case, with interrelated phenomena in time, we are working in the field of determination by causal laws. On the other hand, because of the singularity of historical situations and effects, the establishment of laws and causality in the human and social field is extremely difficult, if not actually impossible. The contingent elements in history cannot be defined in terms of causal laws (of the type whenever such-and-such is the case, so-and-so follows); they can be described only in terms of individual causality (because of this unique constellation of circumstances, the result is so-and-so).

All this goes to show that categorial formulation of the determinations of events under the heading of causality has only limited cognitive significance. In particular, it is in no way superior to the qualitatively specific description of conditioned, stimulated, motivated actions directed towards an end. The advantage in formal stringency gained by the introduction of the principle of causality is bought at the price of increasing the difficulties and doubts surrounding the idea of determination. To say that actions 'plainly and necessarily follow' from the conditions in which they arose (i.e., the combination of the inner mobility of and the external impact upon the acting subject) means taking a great leap over the process that takes place in the acting subject. The grave defect of the causality approach is that determination is regarded as being *determined by*, i.e., as being an essentially passive phenomenon, while it should really be regarded as determined self-determination, or subjective change. To the extent that determination is considered only from the aspect of 'objective happening' and not as a mode of subjective activity, its abstract formulation means disregard, not elucidation, of its essential form. To say that what happened in any particular instance – say, the murder of Liebknecht and Luxemburg in 1919, or Stalin's triumph at the end of the twenties, or Hitler's accession to power in 1933, etc., etc. – was plainly and necessarily bound to happen is as true as it is false. As a reflection of human activity causal observation is actually misleading, because it gives theoretical sanction to the facticity of the outcome. There are good reasons for the fact that the category of causality occupies only a subordinate place in the Marxist view of historical determination.

Historical laws as a fetish

We have seen that Marx gave a prominent place to the idea of historical laws at the time when he was working on the *Critique of Political Economy*. In the development of his theory, however, he did not establish such laws with the thoroughness attributed to him by the reviewer he honoured so signally by quoting. Above all, few statements can be found in his works that can be regarded as statements of general laws of historical development. To that extent the concept of history as a process taking place in accordance with laws remains unproven.

The systematization of historical materialism in the Soviet school of philosophy has not changed this situation greatly, though there is a greater degree of emphasis on social development being based on natural laws, and in particular the idea has been extended to the whole of history. 'The development of society', according to *The Foundations of Marxism-Leninism*, 'is a process that takes place in accordance with laws, subject to definite historical necessity independent of the human consciousness.'[214] The book speaks of a 'process that takes place in accordance with rigid laws', and quotes the words of Marx's reviewer: 'The laws of historical development are objective laws. They are not merely independent of the human will and consciousness, but themselves determine the will, the consciousness and the activity of men.'[215] In spite of this emphasis on laws, however, the book does not do much to amplify the concept of history as a process subject to laws. In so far as the references to laws are not purely verbal – hardly anything trips more lightly from the tongue than these constant references – few statements are made that can be described as statements of historical law. To deduce history from a codification of these laws would be a sheer impossibility. Strictly speaking, everything is made to depend on one single law, the necessity of productive relations being in harmony with the nature of the productive forces. The authors state 'that productive relations change in harmony with the development of the productive forces and that discrepancies arising between them have to be eliminated to allow the productive forces sufficient elbow-room for their development'.[216] That not very much can be deduced from this is obvious enough. When F. Marek claims that Marx deduced from this 'law of movement of history' no less than the inevitability of the socialist revolution, it is a grotesque exaggeration.[217]

The 'nomological' theory of historical materialism as presented by Soviet authors also has other weaknesses. There is no clarity about the working of these laws, or men's relation to them. We have already pointed out that analysis has made it clear that natural laws are patterns of relationship or coordination, but these authors continually make them seem to be something in the nature of forces producing results. Often there is something fetishist about the way in which laws are stated to determine events. In the first place, there are frequent references to the 'effect' of laws, their 'sway' over men, and the 'demands' that they make, and to laws that (in pre-socialist societies) work as blind forces' and degrade men into being their 'slaves'. Laws do not, of course, make history automatically without men playing their part; but they determine the course of history 'over and above' men's actions. Sometimes it is actually stated that laws are themselves a result of human activity and in this capacity determine the general human trend.[218] One is on solid ground, however, in this matter of natural laws only when account is taken of their categorical status and their localization in the context of objective social actions is strictly observed. In other words, laws must be regarded as patterns of coordination and as nothing else. Their 'function' is not directive; the laws of reality are primarily not normative. We are also told that the laws of history, of the historically relevant actions of men, are nothing but definite coordination between men's actions and (1) the initial situation in which they find themselves; (2) the means at their disposal; (3) what others do or are expected to do; (4) the result of the action they take – and many other things as well. The central point round which everything revolves, however, is the concrete, historically determined, socially differentiated behaviour trends of men. However much or little can in this respect be formulated in terms of laws, the only way in which such laws could be stated is as follows: When men belonging to class x find themselves in situation y they behave (invariably or in a definite proportion of cases) in manner z. Human behaviour trends are elementary and fundamental, and in comparison correspondences between characteristics of systems and processes are resultant or derivative. Structural analysis in the field of historical relations among other things invariably means resorting to the coordinates of a 'single teleological assumption' (as Lukács calls it).

But the question is to what extent history can be reduced to the expression of scientific laws. As we have pointed out, situations and behaviour trends are always specific and unique. L. Kofler (like G. Simmel) has sought a way out by postulating 'non-recurring' laws of history.[219] But this leads to logical difficulties and is inherently undesirable. Accordance with law can very well exist when the phenomenon concerned cannot be accounted for by any single law, but is the outcome of an unlimited number of factors all taking place in accordance with law. The domain of the concept of law in its significant sense is that of the isolatable and elementary, the typical and schematic. The individual complexion of a multiplicity of behaviour effects all determined by law cannot generally be identified as a single instance of an overriding general law. Nevertheless – and here lies the way of escape from the doubts and difficulties associated with the individual instance – such an individually constituted phenomenon always betrays general and typical characteristics that with varying degrees of precision can be expressed in terms of law. The fact, of course, must be accepted that in the life of society this is not everything, and in history in particular it is not the decisive factor. Thus we here reach a limitation of the concept of law in history.

It is not only the uniqueness of historical phenomena that imposes this limitation. An, if possible, even more important consideration is that laws describe formal or structural characteristics and always assume the really active factor, as we saw in our discussion of the nomological argument for communism. A law states only how something happens if something else is structured in a particular way. It tells us neither that what is assumed actually takes place nor why the consequence is what it is and not otherwise. In the human social field no less than the whole trend of human self-activity and self-affirmation forms part of this assumption. In reference to this it is fair to say that the hermeneutics of meaning are more important than the formulism of law.

3. DIFFERENT MEANINGS OF NECESSITY

In all discussion of Marxist determinism the idea of necessity rightly occupies a foremost place. The term is anything but unambiguous, but for that very reason does not suffer from the limitations that we detected in the terms causality and law. Its greatest advantage is that it allows, or should allow, the practical meaning of Marxist historical determinism to come into play. Failure to recognize the primarily practical significance of the idea of necessity in Marxism is a grave misunderstanding. It is open to one personally to accept another convention, but it is not consistent with Marxism to follow E. Topitsch in regarding a development as 'necessary' only to the extent that it is insusceptible to human intervention.[220] This concept of necessity, which is taken from natural history, is not the primary one, as A. Brunner correctly points out. 'Necessity', he says, 'is what must happen if disaster is to be averted', and such is the necessity with which we are confronted in the field of history.[221] This, however, is not the only kind of 'necessity' we meet in history; there is also the 'necessity' of an inevitable course of events. Marxist theorists, and above all Marxist propagandists, have certainly encouraged confusion between these two types. J. Habermas calls them practical and theoretical respectively, and one can also talk of the necessity to act and of the necessity of events.

The practical meaning of the word appears most plainly when Marx speaks of the necessity of the emancipation of the proletariat, which, he says, is forced to liberate itself 'by no longer deniable or disguisable, absolutely imperious, need – the practical expression of necessity'.[223] Later Marxist theorists held fast to this practical meaning, as did R. Luxemburg, who in 1918 said: 'Socialism has become a necessity, not merely because the proletariat is no longer willing to live under the living conditions that the capitalist classes are preparing for it, but because, if the proletariat does not fulfil its class duties and achieve socialism, we are all faced with disaster together.'[224] N. Bukharin[225] and A. Gramsci[226] spoke in the same terms. Only at a vulgar level of Marxism can the inevitability of sunset and sunrise and the change of the seasons be used to illustrate the necessity of communism.[227] Modern Soviet textbook philosophy cannot be exonerated of having created little theoretical clarity in the matter. The idea that necessity has two meanings between which it is necessary to distinguish, i.e., inevitability and urgent desirability, was for a long time never mentioned in its compilations.[228]

Three kinds of necessity

Differentiating between the necessity of events and the necessity of action is merely the inescapable minimum. Over and above that, the idea of the necessity of action requires a further step in differentiation. This results in the following:

1. The necessity of events (or *de facto* necessity). The 'necessary' here is a result that follows inevitably from definite initial and marginal conditions. The structural relationship between the elements involved, their co-variance, can be dealt with in isolation as 'nomological necessity'. The necessity of the result is relative to the presence (or non-presence) of the constellation of conditions; its 'inevitability' exists only within the constellation itself, thus it does not necessarily apply to human beings faced with such a course of events.

2. Secondary necessity of action. Here the necessity is a means or method of procedure required for the attainment of an end.

This kind of necessity has, so to speak, two roots. One is based on previous acceptance of the end, and the other on the logical link between the objects and circumstances that serve as means and ends in the context of the action. It is necessity of action of this type that Kant describes as a 'hypothetical imperative'. Here the determination consists of a double and reciprocal relationship of subordination; man, who subordinates means to his end and the causal functioning of things to the object he has set himself, in turn subjects himself to the factual necessity peculiar to the relations of co-variance peculiar to the objective field in which he is working. This is Bacon's *natura parendo vincitur*, which also underlies Engels's phrase about freedom being insight into necessity.

3. Primary subjective necessity of action. Here the necessary is not a means in relation to an end, but is the end itself. It is a primary affirmation, the realization of an end as the satisfaction of a need. Here lies the real source of practical necessity – an obvious or sublime human want, a dissatisfaction or unrest, continually renewed both from without and from within. If the category of values is applied to the things that men use and wish for, this primary necessity can also be called axiological. Necessary activity in this sense is not imposed on men, as is the application of definite means in the necessity directed to an end, but is identical with him; thus Schelling could call it both necessary and 'absolutely free'.

The necessity we classified as secondary is merely a product of the synthesis of primary subjective necessity and the objective necessity of events. A further modification arises in the social inter-subjectivity of men. They jointly make the avoidance of disaster a necessity, and this becomes a categorical imperative. Saying that something is 'necessary' in this sense means that it is in the universal interest.

When we consider Marx's statements about historical necessity in the light of these differences of meaning, it is evident that it is not a single, all-embracing necessity to which he is referring. It has different meanings in the different contexts in which it appears in Marx and Engels. Engels's necessity, insight into which makes one free, is not the same kind of necessity as that which causes men to enter into 'necessary' productive relations, and this differs in turn from the necessity that leads to the 'inevitable' downfall of the capitalist method of production, which again differs from that which will eventually lead to the triumph of socialism. Instead of illustrating this by reference to the texts, we shall quote examples of the typological varieties.

Necessity in historical processes

A first constellation of 'necessity' arises from the 'objective' nature of human activity, that is, from the fact that innumerable elements of external nature play their part in it, both in natural and worked-up form. Natural materials, like tools and other material contrivances, have their own inherent laws. The consequence is that men, who need all these things in order to live, are faced with a multitude of 'hypothetical imperative' necessities. The fact that the great majority of mankind have hitherto had to work so hard and so long in order to live made previous history, as Marx said, a 'realm of necessity'. In so far as all the functions concerned have always been integrated into social contexts, the modes of necessity involved also form part of what can be called social and historical necessity in the narrower sense.

If we look at the actual social process, it seems at first sight perfectly possible in principle to regard it *en bloc* as a natural process in which the later is causally and necessarily the product of the earlier in accordance with underlying natural laws. Nevertheless, in spite of K. R. Popper and others, such an overriding concept of natural causation is in no way significant either for Marxist theory or for Marxist practice. Such an approach is relevant only to limited 'individual processes' and from a quite definite external aspect. If one is dealing with definite constellations of human subjects whose trends are sufficiently plain and whose behaviour is therefore to some extent predictable and over whom one can oneself exercise no modifying influence, it is legitimate to speak of a necessary course of events. The inherent necessity that Marx postulated for the course of development of the capitalist system is of this type. Though in the Marxist view this 'natural' necessity, by which the later is the 'blind' result of the earlier, is not characteristic of the whole process of human history (including future history), it is nevertheless to a high degree characteristic of all 'previous history', to the extent that it in fact took place after the fashion of an irresistible natural process. It is to this that Engels was referring when he spoke of the 'realm of necessity'; necessity is what affects men as if it were fate.

Finally, there is another, even more far-reaching partial aspect of social life in which 'natural necessity' plays a quite outstanding role. Many individual actions and whole courses of action by individuals and groups have this quality of 'natural necessity' within the context of a definite system of behaviour patterns and stereotyped reactions, based, that is to say, on human nature as modified at any particular historical moment. Everything that we said above about the major units of the historical process depends in the last resort on such coordinates. To the extent that such reactive mechanisms are characterized by conditioned necessity, social processes, besides being predictable, are also manageable to the extent that the underlying and marginal conditions are controllable from the outside. Marxist diagnoses and prognoses, not only of the behaviour of capitalists, but also of the system-transcending behaviour of the proletariat, depend on such assessments, based on general and historically modified human nature. To Marx these predictions of behaviour became the starting point for practical communication, for the purpose of providing development aid for the class-consciousness of the proletariat. Elsewhere such behaviour patterns can provide the basis for social engineering manipulations.

So far we have been dealing with a kind of 'natural necessity' in human and social behaviour as it strikes an outside observer. From within, however, a great deal of it appears in the form of a different mode of necessity, that of the 'necessity to act'; the subjects involved behave as they do because they have an essential need of something, or believe they do. Unless a weaker motivation is present, the action that they take is necessary action directed to a vital end. We do not propose to concern ourselves here with particular cases, but with what is inter-subjectively felt to be 'historically necessary' to society as a whole, the practical necessity of historical progress. The extent to which things that are necessary and essential in this practical sense are also 'naturally necessary', in the sense of forming part of an inevitable course of events, is a matter for special consideration. When Marx declared that historical advance, and the advance to communism in particular, was a historical necessity, he was thinking of it primarily as a practical necessity. The position adopted is that something is a practical necessity (i.e., is urgently desirable or vital to life); it may, therefore, also be a necessity of events. It is not the reverse position, that something is a necessity of events and must therefore be pursued as a practical objective, which would result in the logical absurdity pointed out by R. Stammler and the 'double pattern of behaviour' wrongly ascribed to Marxism by E. Topitsch.

4. THE NECESSITY OF PROGRESS

In the context of historical advance various things can be necessary, e.g., definite means and methods of procedure, as well as restrictions and deprivations. But first of all it is necessary to make clear what is meant by the necessity of progress itself; historical advance becomes necessary in practice because men are no longer satisfied with the existing state of affairs in view of the possibilities of a higher level of satisfaction of needs, or see themselves in danger of losing what has already been gained. Thus behind this necessity there lie innate human trends and the expansion of men's subjective needs. In this sense the necessity is subjective, or more correctly, intersubjective. (We believe the time has come definitely to dismiss the defamation of subjectivity and the obsessive idea that there should be an 'objective' criterion for everything that crept in with Stalinism. A Marxist philosophy of practice means, among other things, confirming men in their right to behave subjectively in certain things.)

The necessity of progressive social change is primarily just a 'natural' necessity, the announcement of an imperative requirement and the projection of an urgent goal – the penalty for failing to reach which may possibly be downfall and disaster. The proclamation of the goal, if it is serious and not merely visionary, is essentially a matter, if not of actual, at any rate of potential practical action.

With the problem of realizing the goal the secondary mode of practical necessity that we described above as 'secondary practical' becomes relevant, that is, the necessity of means and methods of procedure. A considerable extra effort in apprehension is required to make concrete decisions ranging from what can be demanded in practice, assessing the opposition, the opportunities of forming alliances, forms of organization, strategy and methods of action, to deciding on the optimal timing for each individual step. It is here that the 'objective factors' in the real meaning of the term have their legitimate place; a multitude of material conditions and objective means are involved in any great social operation. It is, however, unwise in our opinion to dismiss every non-arbitrary factor out of hand as 'objective'.

The methods of procedure necessary to the end aimed at are also primarily a matter of subjective demand and elements in a projection, possibly a controversial one. The 'inherently subjective necessity' of the ends and the course taken by an historical advance do not, however, constitute the 'real' necessity of its success. Marxists agree that in Germany between 1918 and 1923 a revolutionary new beginning was vitally necessary, but in the sense of natural inevitability it was not. An extremely regressive development can in reality also be 'necessary'. We made sufficiently clear above that there can be no ultimate guarantee of success, not even of final and ultimate success. The realization of the practically necessary is achieved by nothing but the character and qualifications of the men committed to it. Historical advance takes place with a quasi-natural necessity only when a sufficient large and qualified number of men, on the basis of their experience with the existing state of affairs as well as an adequate working up of that experience, succeed in developing a strength that is superior to all resistance and, over and above that, is skilfully directed towards the creation of a higher social organization. The necessity of historical progress is always related to concrete situations. After all we have said about historical changes in general, there is no justification for speaking of the necessity of progress in the all-embracing singular, and, above all, the category of necessity must not be hypostasized. Plekhanov, whose thought was greatly influenced by Spinoza, said that it was the Marxist belief that capitalism by the course of its own development would lead to its own negation and the realization of the

Marxist ideal, that this was a historical necessity, and that the Marxist 'served, was bound to serve, wanted to serve, and was bound to want to serve' as one of the tools of that necessity; this was freedom born of necessity, or necessity that had grown into freedom.[229] E. Topitsch quotes this passage to document his criticism of Marxism,[230] but he does not seem to have asked whether this was authentic Marxism. We believe it was not. There is simply no room in it for a necessity that is pre-existent to the acting subject and, so to speak, acts through him, because the practical necessity concerned 'arises out of' the subject in the first place and can be freely identical with him only for that reason. Elbow-room for identification or non-identification exists only to the extent that an individual can withdraw himself from the inter-subjectively constituted practical necessity of common action. It is only in that dimension that anything in the nature of 'service' or 'dedication' is possible; service and dedication, not to necessity or the law of history, but to those who have committed themselves to a struggle and with whom one feels solidarity, though there may be individual chances of evading or escaping from it. An element of moral necessity may lie in that.

Another criticism of Plekhanov's statement is that the self-negation of capitalism is apparently reduced to a single act. In the Marxist view, the downfall of capitalism and the emancipation of the proletariat are two sides of a total process that, as G. Lukács has rightly pointed out, are not mechanically coupled together. Lukács points out that it is fallacious to regard social development as if 'the economic process of capitalism necessarily and automatically led by way of crises to socialism'. He quotes Lenin's view that there is no such thing as an absolutely hopeless situation for capitalism, even if the only 'way out' is a decline into barbarism. The crisis of capitalism in fact results in 'objective possibilities' of a revolutionary solution, though that solution can be 'only the free act of the proletariat itself'.[231] Thus the negative necessities of capitalism are of an order different from that of the affirmative necessity of socialism.

5. NECESSITY AND FREEDOM

From the Marxist viewpoint historical necessity is not anti-
thetical or on a superior plane to human subjectivity; on the
contrary, it is localized in human subjectivity itself. Consequently the problem of freedom and necessity does not arise
in any acute form. (It arises in acute form in relation to the
determination of the individual 'will', but that is a secondary
question from the point of view of the theory of history.) The
other characteristics of practical historical necessity also lead
to no sharp clash with the interests of freedom; historical
necessity, being primarily practical, is not monolithic, but
synthetic; hence everyone is able and entitled to share in
defining it. Being strictly related to circumstances, new efforts
to define and revise it are continually required. In particular,
the choice of means and the establishment of methods of procedure is not firmly laid down. Insight into necessity must be
worked out in wide-ranging controversies; the establishment
of the necessary assumes previous freedom of discussion. Thus
necessity and freedom are in many respects correlative. Also
there is the fact that necessity is not an issue in all historical
projection and realization; it arises only in matters vital to
human and social life. Everything else takes place in the mode
of possibility, and by that very fact in a 'realm of freedom'. It
should be recalled that in Marx's view historical progress tends
increasingly to diminish the realm of necessity in favour of the
realm of freedom.

The idea of freedom has several different meanings, just as
that of necessity has. This has tended to be overlooked, as a
result of Engels's very one-track formula for the coordination
of freedom and necessity, which came to dominate the theoretical
field in the Soviet school. Freedom, Engels said, is insight into
necessity.[232] It is clear from the context that he had in mind a
very special case, namely the freedom of the will in an objective
field determined by natural laws; that is, primarily natural
objects and only secondarily human subject-objects. He was
concerned with the hypothetical imperative of the choice of
means, i.e., with what is necessary in order to gain an end, not
with historical necessity in any all-embracing sense. Neverthe-

less he also said that this adjustment of freedom to necessity applies also to the laws 'that rule the physical and mental life of man itself', and he thus understood freedom as implying control, not only of external nature, but also 'of ourselves'. The Soviet theorists applied Engels's dictum to the 'objective' historical necessity of compact and the overriding 'laws of social development'. Thus necessity was turned into an absolute imperative not derived from humanity itself, and élitarian insight into necessity became a commandment imposed on ordinary mortals to subject themselves to the decision of the experts in the laws of history.

Five The Marxist View of History and the
Historical Present

To Marxists history can serve merely as a guide to the understanding of concrete historical situations and to active intervention in contemporary history. In terms of concrete and
practical history Marxism is the 'theory of the conditions for
the emancipation of the proletariat'.[233] Marx in fact described
his 'original contribution' in more specific terms. He set out
'to show (1) that the existence of classes is connected with
definite historical phases of development of production; (2)
that the class struggle necessarily leads to the dictatorship of the
proletariat; (3) that the latter merely provides the transition to
the abolition of all classes and to a classless society'.[234] Thus
the general concept of history is concretized in a definite concept of the historical present as history to be made.

For many years there has been discussion whether and to what
extent the Marxist theory of history has stood up to the test of
the present age and can continue to serve as a basis for historical
projections. Apart from innumerable details, debate has centred
on the Marxist theories about the general historical prospect of
the supersession of class society by the revolutionary self-
liberation of the workers and on the historical materialist view
of the connection between material production and the life of
society in general. In all this there is always the question which of
the Marxist theories and prognoses are essential for the theory
as a whole and which are to be regarded merely as hypotheses
subject to revision.

Many refutations of Marx have been offered. It has been
pointed out that the revolution he declared to be inevitable has
failed to take place where, according to his predictions, it should
have taken place, and that instead it has taken place where,

according to him, it should not have happened at all; and that a 'Marxist' society has been established that not only has 'not yet' reached the Marxist goal of a classless, free society, but is possibly not even on the way to it. What facts and considerations can therefore be brought forward in Marx's favour?

We shall confine ourselves to matters bearing on the concept of history. When one thinks in terms of history, there is a primary methodical principle to be borne in mind – the necessity of exercising due restraint in drawing up 'final' balance-sheets. Our difficulties with Marxism (and the difficulties of Marxism with itself) are to a large extent a quite usual instance of the general difficulty of thinking in historical periods instead of in terms of one's own life-span. The time for a final balance-sheet of Marx's great historical projection has simply not yet come. The fact that he himself reckoned in much shorter periods of time is the least weighty of the arguments against him. The establishment of bourgeois society was spread over several centuries, but there seemed to be some evidence to show that it would very quickly reach the limits of its possibilities and that the socialist transformation, though it was to be far more deep-reaching than earlier revolutions, might be achieved by the work of two or three generations. Marx and Engels had to correct themselves in their own lifetime, after the 1848 revolution, and today, about 125 years after the first great correction, comfort can be gained from what Marx said at the time – that another fifteen, twenty or fifty years of civil and national wars might be needed before the old world was destroyed and the founders of the new world had grown ripe for it.

I. THEORETICAL CONSTANTS AND VARIABLES

The implications of historical materialism for the understanding of the present phase of history can be summarized as follows:

1. The general outlook. Because of the high and increasing productivity of industrial technique, it is possible in principle to provide mankind so amply with the means of existence, and so greatly to reduce the social differences between men and the distance between nations, that exploitation, domination and lethal conflict can completely and finally be eliminated from social life.

2. The conflict situation. The higher possibilities of human existence are not achieved automatically. Instead, the productive forces leading in the direction of higher development (i.e., primarily the producers) come into conflict with existing productive relations (which are defended by the ruling class), resulting in a crisis that manifests itself in the productive forces acting as destructive forces.

3. The ways toward a solution. The conflict has to be fought out in political struggle between social classes, and the outcome is progressive if the oppressed class is not only obliged by the pressures and renunciations imposed on it to fight for emancipation, but also and over and above that embodies in its social situation and its activity the principles of order of a different method of production.

4. The chances of a solution. The supersession of class differences, which is the purpose of the socialist transformation of society, is a long drawn out process, the progress of which essentially depends on the development of the material productive forces of society.

These positions were surrounded by continually changing situations in Marx's and Engels's lifetime, and they remained so throughout the further history of Marxism. Some of these positions became important to the history of socialism and the current view of Marxism. (1) The conflict situation that in the classical Marxist texts points the way to the crisis of capitalist production is a very simple model, based on few coordinates. According to this model, in all the capitalist industrial countries a central conflict between bourgeoisie and proletariat develops, drawing its energy from the permanent pressure on the working class and in particular from the periodic upheavals of the inevitable economic crises, which tend to grow from bad to worse. (2) The classical Marxist texts foresee a relatively rectilinear development of the crisis of the capitalist system and a parallel development of the revolutionary socialist workers' movement. (3) Marx assumed that the crisis of capitalism would first reach its climax in the most highly developed industrial nations and lead to the socialist revolution.

It is of course an easy task to dismiss this 'Marxism' as a tremendous over-simplification of the complex historical reality of our time. It should, however, be noted that the elements of a far more complex theory are to be found in Marx and Engels (particularly in their political statements and statements on contemporary events), and above all that Marxism does not have to be rigidly limited to the summary statements of principle that have gained acceptance in current interpretations of Marxism.

1. In the early writings on historical materialism the idea of capitalism as a world-wide system makes its appearance, soon to be followed by the insight that developments in the highly developed industrial countries are dependent on those on the periphery, the undeveloped areas. After 1848 international relations, particularly those between the European powers, came within the purview of Marxist strategy, and after the Franco-German war of 1870-1 international power politics and the international workers' movement were in Marx's and Engels's view inseparably connected. In an 1890 letter Engels expressed the opinion that developments were leading to a world war or world revolution (or a combination of the two).[235] Hence it was merely a logical step that the imperialist world system should become the frame of reference of the Marxist theory of imperialism.

2. With the extension of the frame of reference, the system of coordinates of capitalist 'contradictions' and conflicts became more complicated. In the twentieth century purely economic crises (besides appearing in modified form) have been over-shadowed by the huge national wars of the imperialist system. On top of this, social and political struggles took place in the undeveloped countries, in the social structure of which poor and oppressed peasants played an important part and became active as revolutionary potential. Finally, struggles began between imperialist colonial powers and suppressed peoples that were socially on the move.

3. The crises in the capitalist world consequently took a course different from that which Marx thought probable. Marx, thinking in terms of the few capitalist industrial nations (he was specifically discussing the relations between Britain and Germany), said that the industrially more developed country showed the less developed merely the picture of its own future. But what actually happened was that the semi-developed or entirely undeveloped countries of the capitalist periphery that

were hungry for development saw in the capitalist homelands the picture of a future that was closed to them. This made them take the more hardly destructive effects resulting from the activities of the leading capitalist powers. The consequence was that revolutionary centres arose in areas where the existing social order – a mixture of pre-capitalist, early capitalist and foreign capitalist elements – had already exhausted the specific local possibilities of development at a very low level of industrialization. True, it is a principle of historical materialism that a social system does not succumb 'before all the productive forces have been developed for which it is broad enough', but it is nowhere stated that any particular type of method of production everywhere possesses the same 'breadth' of possibilities. Thus the negative and positive preconditions for a socialist revolution can vary very widely. This gives a special character to the process of its international development.

4. One 'fact' that is said to weigh very heavily against Marx does not put a question-mark against any of his theories, but confirms one of his gloomiest fears, in that it struck a practical blow at what he stood for. The fact that the capitalist social order in its homelands has been able to survive the upheavals of our century is above all attributable to the fact that the possibility presented itself on a gigantic scale of diverting the energy of unfulfilled social demand from the field of social conflicts into other channels – those of nationalist, racial and imperialist aggression and identifications. Marx became acutely aware of the danger of such 'displacement' of the potential or historical conflict when the victorious Prussian Germany of 1870 helped itself to a slice of French territory. This, he wrote, after a short interval would lead to another war, a 'racial war' (in extent, not content) against the allied Slavs and Latins. Writing to the branches of the International, he said: 'If the workers forget their duty, if they remain passive, the present terrible war will only be the predecessor of still more terrible international struggles and will lead in every country to new defeats of the workers by the gentlemen of the sword, landed property and capital.'[236] After that chauvinism increasingly spread until the Socialist International capitulated to it in 1914. Anti-Semitism, often encouraged by the authorities to counter the socialist workers' movement, handed the Jews over to aggression arising

from social injustices. All this reached its climax in German Nazism – a great deal of which still continues in the form of anti-communism and hostility to revolutionary movements in the Third World. Our quotation from Marx shows that he did not regard the development of anti-capitalist class-consciousness among the oppressed as an irresistible 'automatic development', but as something that would have to be fought for in a hard struggle with many vicissitudes.

2. CAPITALISM A CENTURY AFTER 'CAPITAL'

The development of bourgeois society did not in fact lead to the tremendous simplification of the socialist problem of which the *Communist Manifesto* spoke. But can it be claimed that the problem raised by Marx has been solved, or that it has been displaced by another that cannot be dealt with in the terms of Marxist theory? Neither is the case. The problems that are generally referred to in Marxist terminology under the heading of the contradictions of capitalism, instead of duly coming to a head, have changed and shifted their ground, contrary to Marx's expectations, but, so far from fading away, have intensified, and to a large extent have remained unsolved; the problems of the productive forces and productive relations, and of the productive and the destructive forces, and of social antagonisms are still with us. It must be admitted that Marx had an insufficient idea of the extent of the negativity inherent in the existing order. What he in his time regarded as an indication of the necessity of a 'fundamental revolution' nowadays seems trifling in the light of the catastrophes of the first half of the twentieth century. The 'modern industrial society' of organized capitalism remains to a high degree a repressive system of discipline and privilege, of authority and rivalry relations, a system of high liability and susceptibility to crisis, with a large amount of potential for internal conflict and precarious external relations, a huge deficit of elementary enlightenment and a tremendous amount of applied anti-enlightenment. The trends to action in international relations and conflicts remain those of the traditional class society; there is no sign of any new quality beyond that of imperialism.

In the light of this situation it is idle to claim that the problems of bourgeois society discovered by Marx have been settled. The favourite evidence produced to show social satisfaction in the highly developed countries – the higher wages, though they are still not so very high, and the not very substantial guarantees behind them, some advances in the social field, and an economic policy that since the end of the Second World War has been able to keep recessions within certain bounds – are not convincing.[237] These things merely show that there is no rectilinear process of decline and 'collapse' of the capitalist system, no staggering from one devastating crisis to the next, each more devastating than the last, and no rectilinear trend to an ever-increasing 'impoverishment' of the workers. But Marxism was never based on such expectations. According to the Marxist theory of history, it would seem much more probable that social crisis would manifest itself at irregular intervals and in different social spheres.

If we abide by the fundamental Marxist criteria for the diagnosis of a society, the questions to be asked in relation to the capitalist world system of the present day are as follows: Are the productive relations of the social, political and cultural systems for the reproduction of that society optimal, or at least adequate, forms of development for the material, social and cultural productive forces of humanity in the twentieth century? Are the productive forces in these conditions adequate to their human content, or are they still in danger of working as destructive forces? Are social antagonisms so resolved that the class struggle of the controlled against the controllers has come to an end, or has been reduced to routine conflicts? All these questions can be very categorically answered. The conflict between the social purpose of production and private capitalist appropriation is far from having been resolved by the amount of national and international economic coordination that characterizes organized capitalism. Both the international cooperation of highly industrialized countries and the development of the backward countries call for all-embracing socialist economic planning and relations of socialist solidarity between the nations of the world. There is no need to mention the predominance that the destructive forces have gained over the requirements of human life; and finally, if the capitalist world system in its homelands has so far survived the catastrophes of our age, that is an extremely ambiguous achievement. It is only partially to be ascribed to the circumstance that the capitalist economy has demonstrated a capacity over fairly long periods to solve in relatively tolerable fashion the problem of satisfying some of the elementary needs of important sections of the working population. The chief share in responsibility for the survival of the system is due, not to the fashion in which it has avoided conflicts, but to that in which it has perverted them and reproduced itself by way of that perversion. It took refuge, so to speak, from the class struggle in two world wars, and gained some benefit for itself by using the first anti-capitalist revolution to restrain and divert inner conflicts. The great extent to which this was possible is one of the lessons of history that twentieth-century Marxism has to learn. But responsibility for the fact that it was possible must to a large extent be ascribed to the socialist leadership, with whom lies the ultimate responsibility for the practical outcome of the crises of the capitalist world system.

3. PROSPECTS OF THE ANTI-CAPITALIST MOVEMENT

Even in Marx's and Engels's lifetime the union of the proletarians of all countries in the struggle against the domination of capital was far from being a triumphal march. What Marx wrote about the phenomenology of the proletarian movement must be remembered and transposed to an even greater historical scale. 'Proletarian revolutions . . . constantly criticize themselves, continually interrupt themselves in their own course, go back on what they have apparently accomplished in order to start from the beginning again, ridicule with cruel thoroughness the half measures, weaknesses and pitifulnesses of their first attempts, throw their enemy with the only result that he seems to gather new strength from the ground and rises again to confront them in even more gigantic form, continually recoil from the vague enormity of their own aims, until a situation has been created that makes any turning back impossible and conditions themselves declare: *Hic Rhodus, hic salta.*'[238] Premature and superficial claims are often made nowadays to the effect that we have seen the end of the proletarian movement and the proletarian class struggle. But what reason is there in principle to believe that the socialist movement in the countries that are still capitalist are not merely going through a crisis in which they are having to work out the consequences of the defeats they have suffered and the new situation brought about by organized capitalism? It cannot be maintained that there is an advanced and definitive satisfaction of social needs, or that there is an absence of social conflict in which the interests of large groups clash. The situation is rather that the latent potential of social conflict is still very great, and that it depends to a large extent on purposeful organizational initiative how this will become manifest. In comparison with Marx's time the social basis for social clashes has actually notably broadened.

The Marxism of the Second and Third Internationals was ideologically concentrated on the figure of the factory worker, and this was its historical limitation. Highly qualified groups of producers who can be described as the new working class, though from the organizational point of view little headway has been made among them, have entered the field of vision of present-day socialist strategy. 'In fact', S. Mallet writes, 'the greater the increase in the importance of the sectors of research, planning and supervision, the greater the concentration of human labour on the preparation and organization of production, the greater the growth of the sense of initiative and responsibility, the more, in short, does the modern worker at the collective level regain the occupational autonomy that he lost in the phase of the mechanization of labour, and the more will he develop the tendency to take a share in control.' Here we have not only a 'strong arm' that can bring all the wheels to a standstill, but also a whole complex of abilities that can show the way and build the future in a totally different fashion. It is fallacious to regard the 'social question' as settled because only a few marginal groups suffer from severe material want. Higher needs, particularly in connection with only slight variations in the satisfaction of elementary needs, can develop the same energy that grows from material need at lower levels.

4. THE HISTORICAL PROBLEM OF THE UNPLANNED AND UNCOMPLETED REVOLUTION

To many the most awkward of all the 'refutations' of Marx at the present day lies in the very place where (at any rate according to the official creed) Marx himself became an accomplished fact –

i.e., the Russian October Revolution and its consequences. The question is not only what that revolution means to the prospect of human emancipation, but also what is its legitimacy in the light of the principles of historical materialism (or alternatively, what is the legitimacy of those principles in the light of that revolution). Let us begin with this last point. According to A. Gramsci, the Bolshevik revolution was a contradiction of Marx's *Capital* and shattered the creed of historical materialism.[239] The difficulty is obviously that a relatively backward country was the first to set about making the socialist transformation. Not only did this seem to throw to the winds Marx's and Engels's plain warnings that a high degree of development of the material productive forces was required for the socialist revolution, because otherwise the result would only be that 'all the old filth' would be resurrected again;[240] it also conflicted with the whole trend of historical materialism because, according to the actual order of events in the historical process, it should not have been possible for a less developed country to show the more highly developed countries a picture of their own revolution (instead of the reverse, as Marx taught). Thus it looked as if one must either join Marx in discrediting Lenin or use Lenin to reduce Marx to absurdity.

We consider this argument to be fallacious, because it adequately reflects neither the basic theoretical principles of materialism nor the coordinates of the historical situation in 1917.

1. Historical materialism is not a technological determinism endowed with the stringency of mathematics. Material productive forces do not of themselves produce social orders, etc., but put various possibilities at men's disposal, the only limitations on these possibilities being material limitations. Furthermore, historical materialism is not a logic of what can be attempted, but a logic of what can be accomplished. It tells us nothing about what happens or 'must' happen, but indicates (very elastically) certain correlations in the field of possibility of social action, and points to conditions that must be taken into account. Historical materialism is not a mathematics of social construction, but provides bearings in a field that is only incompletely calculable. Marx points out that 'world history would indeed be very easy to make if the struggle were taken up only when conditions were infallibly favourable'.[241]

2. It was of course very clear to Lenin in 1917 that Russia was not exactly amply provided with the positive material and cultural prerequisites for socialism. But his practical calculations helped him over the stile. For one thing, he pointed out, no one could say exactly what the prerequisites for socialism were, and at any rate some of them were present in Russia. For another, this was not the only consideration in such a hopeless, desperate situation, in which a return to 'normal bourgeois conditions' was unthinkable and the overriding need of the hour was to find a new way. 'What about a people that found itself in a revolutionary situation such as that created during the first imperialistic war?' he wrote. 'Might it not, influenced by the hopelessness of its situation, fling itself into a struggle that would offer it at least some chance of securing conditions for further development of civilization that were somewhat unusual?' The historical materialist principle that a form of development for the productive forces has to be found is discernible here in a variant highly specific to its time and place. But, since such further development in the direction of socialism seemed to be practicable only in transitional forms, something else in relation to historical materialism seemed to be involved – a 'modification', a reversal of the 'usual historical order'. 'If a definite level of culture is required for the building of socialism ... why cannot we begin', Lenin continued, 'by first achieving the prerequisites for that definite level of culture in a revolutionary way, then ... with the aid of ... the Soviet system proceed to overtake the other nations?'[242] By this, he believed, the general line of development of world history would not be fundamentally altered – in any case what textbook laid down that such modifications were impossible or inadmissible? Finally, he courageously admitted that, notwithstanding all this, he had taken a chance; he quoted Napoleon's saying: *On s'engage et puis on voit*, and when he dictated these sentences he felt he had found himself. In other statements dating from that time he was less confident.[242]

3. A decisive factor in Lenin's strategic calculations that is not mentioned in the above quotation was the connection of the Russian Revolution with the revolutionary prospects in western and central Europe. So long as the hope of an early 'German October revolution' remained alive, the question of sequence

in the development of the international revolution seemed secondary. It was not the prematurity of the Russian Revolution, but the collapse and fade-out of the western European revolution that was the historical scandal.

All in all, we believe it to be wrong to claim that the October Revolution defied the canon of historical materialism. Lenin did not make history in a way that lay outside 'Marxist legitimacy'; he was not more 'wilful' than Marx, and the amount of will that he put to work did not exceed the amount that historical materialism regards as usual in historical initiatives. What is true is that on the scale of historical possibilities this revolution did not take place in optimal conditions, and this both limited its emancipatory effect on the one hand and on the other increased the chances of counter-movements hostile to emancipation.

This brings us to another question, the meaning of the Russian Revolution in the light of the prospects of human emancipation. There can be no question here of drawing up a final balance-sheet that would include what may be possible in the future; and a further reason for restraint is that no one can say what the alternatives to the Bolshevik revolution might have been.[243] Hence the chief question is whether the sequence of subsequent events was the optimum within the field of historical possibilities. We believe (with I. Deutscher) that the provisional balance-sheet of this 'uncompleted revolution' is full of contradictions, that, side by side with tremendous achievements in construction on the broadest base, terrible destruction has been wrought, and that the rehabilitation of the revolution is advancing only slowly. The negative side of this balance-sheet presents problems that cannot be as casually dismissed as they generally are by Lenin's epigoni. The beginnings of social democracy quickly collapsed, the dictatorship became universal and autocratic, and even after the elimination of the mass terrorism of the Stalin era a system of rigid disciplining of society by the apparatus of the ruling group persisted. The development of social democracy lags behind the development of the material productive forces. The extent of this negative side is strikingly illustrated by the antagonisms that have broken out in the 'socialist world system'.

From the point of view of the Marxist theory of history, the more soberly one looks at the negative side of the emancipatory balance-sheet of the Russian revolution, the more pertinently there arises the question of how 'necessary' it was that everything should have come about in the way it did. In communist oppositional groups the question is continually discussed (L. Trotsky, A. Thalheimer). Let us look at I. Deutscher's résumé of these discussions. He begins with a massive statement of the element of historical necessity in the course of Soviet history, and he quotes G. M. Trevelyan, who answered a similar problem in regard to the Great Rebellion as follows: 'Men were what they were, uninfluenced by the belated wisdom of posterity and they acted. Whether or not any better way could have led to the same end . . .'[244] Deutscher too, after weighing up the historical circumstances, continually comes to the conclusion that things were bound to turn out as they did in Russia; the logic of the situation imposed itself and gave short shrift to oppositional ideas and scruples.[245] But, judging historical situations as a politician, he does not allow himself to be pinned down to such 'objectivism' in relating what happened as if it were inevitably necessary. 'But it may be held, as I have held through all these decades, that without the violence, the blood, and the tears the great work of construction might have been more efficiently carried out and, with healthier social, political and moral after-effects.'[246] (Deutscher also regards the defeats of socialism in the west as not having been historically inevitable.)[247]

'Necessity' here means that, granted existing human behaviour trends, no other outcome was possible in the existing circumstances. If one approves of the final outcome of the process, necessity easily acquires a practical implication, i.e., that in order to attain that end the whole process, including its shady side, is (or was) necessary. The judgement is global, and a general or particular amnesty covers the negative side of the balance-sheet. Lenin rejected such 'objectivism' and called for differentiated analysis of historical events from a particular point of view, just as Marx and Engels attacked 'objective history writing' that considered historical relations in isolation from human activity.[248] Marxism here means having a practical and not merely contemplative attitude to past history. In historical retrospect one continually comes across persons and groups whose activities promised the avoidance, or at any rate the minimization, of certain evils. Retrospective solidarity with them has prospective importance; it is an element in the practice of self-responsible participation in history, in contrast to mere falling in with a 'trend'.

It is possible to develop a line of argument according to which what actually happened was the only thing that could have happened. But such a view of natural necessity eliminates all the dialectical tension associated with the phenomenon of action as distinct from mere happening (and letting things happen). Action is thus understood (or rather misunderstood to be) a continuation of movement already taking place. Arguing on these lines is an indication of deficient practice. Theoretical analysis does not lead to an affirmation of natural necessity in history that is elevated to the normative plane by that affirmation, but to the reaffirmation of a concept of history as a field of limited possibilities which one's own action plays a part in defining.

From this aspect, the Soviet revolution presents itself as a permanent sequence of greater and smaller opportunities of making the best possible use of unfavourable conditions. It was not the inevitable consequence of a process set in train by the upheaval of 1917, by the view of the functions of the party taken by Lenin in 1902, or by any deficiency in Marxist humanism. Step by step, and in a manner that can be concretely determined and criticized in each case, the leadership of the revolution fell short of the possible, not only in doing what was actually possible, but also in hindering negative developments. A 'perfect' socialist democracy was indeed impossible, but the progressive destruction of internal party democracy after 1921 and its culmination in the Stalinist autocracy was not based on any strict logic of the situation, but on more specific variables. In particular, it was not inevitable that the international communist movement should share so catastrophically in the loss of revolutionary spontaneity by which Soviet Russia was affected. It is always a question of from whom one takes one's standards – those who allegedly or really could not do otherwise, or those who showed that it is perfectly possible to do so.

Notes

1. L. Kofler, *Der proletarische Bürger*, 1964, pp. 246–7.
2. O. K. Flechtheim, *Zur Kritik der Marxschen Geschichtskonzeption, Cahiers Vilfredo Pareto*, no. 5, 1965, pp. 141–58.
3. *Werke*, Dietz-Ausgabe, 1958 ff., vol. 1, pp. 338–9.
4. *Werke*, Supplementary vol. 1, pp. 544, 546, 579, 570, 542.
5. ibid., p. 540.
6. ibid., pp. 536 (591–2).
7. O. K. Flechtheim, op. cit., p. 145, n. 2.
8. H. Zeltner, *Ideologie und Wahrheit: Zur Kritik der politischen Vernunft*, 1966, p. 29.
9. E. Topitsch, *Vom Ursprung und Ende der Metaphysik*, 1958, p. 255.
10. R. Tucker, *Karl Marx: Die Entwicklung seines Denkens von der Philosophie zum Mythos*, 1963, p. 20.
11. K. Löwith, *Weltgeschichte und Heilsgeschehen. Die theologischen Voraussetzungen der Geschichtsphilosophie*, 1953, p. 48.
12. In the introduction to *Zur Kritik der Hegelschen Rechtsphilosophie, Werke*, vol. 1, p. 379.
13. *Werke*, vol. 2, p. 98.
14. *Werke*, vol. 3, p. 69.
15. ibid., p. 37.
16. ibid., p. 45.
17. ibid., p. 71.
18. *Werke*, vol. 13, p. 9.
19. *Grundrisse der Kritik der politischen Ökonomie*, 1953, p. 387.
20. In the final sentences of *Poverty of Philosophy*, *Werke*, vol. 4, p. 182.
21. *Umrisse zu einer Kritik der Nationalökonomie*, *Werke*, vol. 1, p. 515.
22. *Werke*, vol. 20, pp. 323–4.
23. ibid., p. 264.

24. *Werke*, vol. 3, p. 45.
25. ibid., p. 28.
26. ibid., p. 29.
27. ibid., p. 72.
28. ibid., p. 38.
29. ibid., pp. 37–8. This passage makes it clear how erroneous it is to regard Engels's later letters on historical materialism as a withdrawal from earlier positions. The comments on totality and reciprocal interaction were inserted by Marx into the manuscript drafted by Engels; thus these letters cannot be regarded as critical of Marx.
30. ibid., p. 30.
31. ibid., p. 27.
32. ibid., pp. 35, 37, 60.
33. ibid., p. 37. The social power resulting from the cooperation of individuals under conditions of division of labour 'seems to those individuals ... to be not their own, united power, but an alien one; they do not know where it comes from or where it is going, and so they cannot control it; on the contrary it is a strange power, independent of men's will and activity, and actually goes through a series of phases and levels of development that controls their will and activity' (p. 34). This anticipates a formulation that will concern us later in connection with the Marxist concept of historical laws.
34. ibid., p. 35.
35. They said that productive forces had turned into destructive forces; that a revolutionary class had arisen; that other people were interested in the preservation of the *status quo*; that the communist revolution involved the abolition of classes; and that the revolutionary class would rid itself of all the old mischief only by a revolution (pp. 69–70).
36. ibid., p. 6.
37. A. Schaff, *Marxismus und das menschliche Individuum*, 1965, p. 84.
38. J. M. Bochenski, *Die kommunistische Ideologie und die Würde; Freiheit und Gleichheit der Menschen*, 1956, pp. 25–7.
39. L. Althusser, *Pour Marx*, 1966, pp. 233–4.
40. Marx criticizes Wagner for not having noticed 'that my analytical method, that proceeds not from man, but from the economically given social period, has nothing in common with the German professorial method of linking ideas'. *Werke*, vol. 19, p. 371.
41. cf. the posthumous introduction to the *Critique of Political Economy*, *Werke*, vol. 13.

42. K. Korsch, *Karl Marx*, 1967, pp. 136–7.

43. cf. the parallel passage in the introduction to the *Critique of Hegel's Philosophy of Law*, in which he says that 'the foundation of irreligious criticism is that man makes religion, and that religion does not make man. True, religion is the self-consciousness of man who has not yet acquired himself or has lost himself again. But man is not an abstraction, a being existing outside the world. Man is the world of men, the state, society. This state, this society, produce religion, a distorted world consciousness, because it is a distorted world.' *Werke*, vol. 1, p. 378.

44. This notion occurs in a footnote in *Capital*, *Werke*, vol. 23, p. 637.

45. *Grundrisse der Kritik der politischen Ökonomie*, p. 157.

46. *Wagner Randglossen*, *Werke*, vol. 19, pp. 362–3.

47. H. Marcuse, in a 1935 paper, 'Zum Begriff des Wesens', *Zeitschrift für Sozialforschung*, vol. 5, no. 1, criticizes the lack of specificity of such a concept of being. But it is precisely the lack of specificity and disjunctivity of such a concept of being that enables it to be maintained. So far as definite postulates are concerned, these are best dealt with under another heading.

48. E. Fromm, *Das Menschenbild bei Marx*, 1963, p. 33.

49. *Werke*, vol. 8, p. 115.

50. *Werke*, vol. 21, pp. 296–7.

51. ibid., p. 298.

52. *Grundrisse der Kritik der politischen Ökonomie*, p. 176.

53. 'In the social production of their lives men enter into definite, necessary, relations that are independent of their will, productive relations that correspond to a definite stage of development of their material productive forces. The totality of these productive relations forms the economic structure of society, the real basis on which a juridical and political superstructure arises, and which correspond to definite forms of social consciousness. . . . At a certain stage of their development the material productive forces of society come into conflict with the existing productive relations . . . with the property relations within which they have hitherto moved. These relations are transformed from forms of development of the productive forces into shackles on them. A period of social revolution then sets in.' *Werke*, vol. 13, pp. 8–9.

54. K. Korsch, op. cit., p. 136.

55. *Werke*, vol. 23, p. 16.

56. *Werke*, vol. 3, pp. 74–7.

57. *Werke*, supplementary vol. 1, pp. 518–19. This return to an original alienation between individuals and groups qualifies what Marx says later about alienated labour as inherently creating alienation from itself, its product and its master ('who does not produce'). The relationship cannot initially establish itself but at most can reproduce itself in this way.

58. *Werke*, vol. 1, pp. 514–15.

59. *Werke*, vol. 3, p. 72.

60. *Werke*, vol. 21, p. 297.

61. *Werke*, vol. 23, pp. 15–16.

62. Engels, *Anti-Dühring, Werke*, vol. 20, p. 264.

63. cf. A. Schmidt, *Der Begriff der Natur in der Lehre von Marx*, 1962, pp. 33–4; T. W. Adorno, *Negative Dialektik*, 1966, p. 246.

64. *Werke*, vol. 23, p. 26. cf. the passage in the *German Ideology* quoted in note 31.

65. The authors of a recent compilation, V. Kelle and M. Koval-zon, go so far in the autonomization of this concept as to devote more than 100 pages to it, only to reach the conclusion that actual history is 'the result of the activity of men'.

66. ibid., vol. 23, p. 12.

67. ibid., p. 16.

68. ibid., p. 12.

69. ibid., p. 27.

70. *Werke*, vol. 19, p. 335.

71. L. Kofler, *Der proletarische Bürger*, p. 246.

72. E. Bloch, *Das Prinzip Hoffnung*, 1959, pp. 84 ff.

73. *Osnovy marksistskoj filosofi*, first Russian edition, 1958. Henceforward we quote the German edition of 1960, to which the page numbers in brackets refer.

74. Meanwhile a good deal of criticism of this has emerged among Soviet philsophers. cf. in particular G. S. Batiščev, 'Man's Active Nature as a Philosophical Principle' ('Dejatel'naja suščnost čeloveka kak filosofkij princip'), 1966, in the proceedings of a conference, and in a shorter version in *Voprosy filosofii*, 1967, no. 3. This author admits no 'factors' in relation to which men are 'products'.

75. *Grundlagen der Marxistischen Philosophie*, p. 392. P. Bollhagen points out, however, that the laws of society are never independent of the activity of men. 'On the contrary, the laws themselves are the objective result of the activity of men and, for their part, when they have been formed, are the objective preconditions of human activity' (*Inceresse und Gesellsceaft*, 1967,

p. 30). This, however, is still incorrect in our opinion, for laws are neither a product nor a precondition.

76. P. Bollhagen points out that the difficulties with the idea of 'interest' into which the author of a Soviet work on historical materialism gets when he states: 'Every interest is in the last resort the expression of economic relations . . . interest is an objective relationship that expresses the specificity of the effect of social laws' (op. cit., p. 21).

77. T. W. Adorno, *Negative Dialektik*, p. 76.

78. W. Maltusch, *Materielles Interesse als Motive. Triebkräfte sozialistischer Produktion philosophisch sowie kybernetisch untersucht*, 1966, p. 9. H. Seidel delivered a massive attack on the objectivist errors underlying the traditional doctrine in 'Vom praktischen und theoretischen Verhältnis der Menschen zur Wirklichkeit', *Deutsche Zeitschrift für Philosophie*, 1966, no. 10, thus sparking off a vigorous controversy. The Soviet philosopher V. P. Tugarinov has pleaded for a broadening of the repertoire of the categories of historical materialism on the subjective side. cf. his *Theory of Values in Marxism* (*Teorija cennostej v marksizme*), 1968. The need for a theory of human activity is now widely felt.

79. *Gespräche mit Georg Lukács*, 1967, p. 60.

80. Letter to P. W. Annenkow (1846), *Werke*, vol. 4, p. 548.

81. *Grundrisse der Kritik der politischen Ökonomie*, p. 157.

82. E. Bloch, *Das Prinzip Hoffnung*, pp. 75–6.

83. Critics continually assume that Marx denies any universal human nature or reduces it to historically variable social relations. (P. C. Ludz, 'Karl Marx', *De homine*, ed. M. Landmann, 1962, p. 480, though the opposite appears from the text; A. Brunner, *Geschichtlichkeit*, 1961, p. 157.)

84. L. Kofler, *Der asketische Eros*, 1967, pp. 25–9. Since the completion of the present work a new work by Kofler, *Perspektiven des revolutionären Humanismus*, 1968, has appeared in which he puts forward a number of anthropological characteristics (physical organization, psychical organization, reasoning ability, capacity for planned action, sociability, historicity, polarity of the self and social ties). We would not, however, limit the concept of the 'anthropological' to such constants, but would include under it observation of historical modifications in so far as this is carried out from the viewpoint of their reflecting different manifestations of man and his way of being.

85. O. Šik, *Ökonomie-Interessen-Politik*, 1966, p. 309. 'The aspiration to live in freedom and not in a cage is characteristic of

every living creature' (V. P. Tugarinov, *Über die Werte des Lebens und der Kultur*, vol. 4, p. 200).

86. Thus Marx once said: 'The proletariat that does not wish to be treated as rabble has even greater need of its spirit, its self-feeling, its pride and its sense of independence than it has of its bread' (*Werke*, vol. 4, p. 200).

87. *Werke*, vol. 25, p. 828.

88. *Werke*, supplementary vol. 1, p. 517.

89. ibid., p. 309. M. Horkheimer, 'Geschichte und Psychologie', *Zeitschrift für Sozialforschung*, Year 1, 1932, p. 139, wrote: 'At all events, the actions of men do not spring merely from the impulse to physical self-preservation or merely from the direct sexual instinct, but also, for instance, from the need to activate the aggressive forces, besides the need for recognition and confirmation of the individual personality, as well as the need for shelter within a group and other impulses besides.'

90. cf. P. Bollhagen, *Interesse und Gesellschaft*, pp. 25, 60 ff.

91. E. Fromm, *Das Menschenbild bei Marx*, pp. 22–3, goes too far when he claims that the basic premise of historical materialism has nothing to do with a basic economic impulse. Only a page earlier he grants the essential point that the determining function of the method of production had a 'quasi-psychological' premise, men's need of food, shelter, etc.

92. As K. Kautsky, *Die materialistische Geschichtsauffassung*, vol. 1, pp. 56, rightly points out, the chief point is not economic motivation, but economic conditioning.

93. *Grundrisse der Kritik der politischen Ökonomie*, p. 387.

94. E. Bloch, *Naturrechte und menschliche Würde*, 1961, p. 237.

95. In the *Critique of Hegel's Philosophy of Law* (*Werke*, vol. 1, p. 385) he speaks of 'doing away with all conditions in which man is a humiliated, enslaved, abandoned, despised creature'.

96. *Werke*, vol. 20, pp. 168–9, 262–3.

97. *Werke*, vol. 1, p. 516.

98. *Werke*, vol. 25, p. 828.

99. H. Marcuse believes that the difference between the two realms may soon disappear (*Das Ende der Utopie*, p. 12, and his paper at the International Summer School at Korčula, Yugoslavia, 1968).

100. A. Schmidt, 'Über Geschichte und Geschichtsschreibung in der materialistischen Dialektik', *Folgen einer Theorie, Essays über 'Das Kapital' von Karl Marx*, 1967, p. 111.

101. G. Del Vecchio, 'Kritik der materialistischen Geschichtsauffassung', *Zeitschrift für philosophische Forschung*, vol. 3, 1965, p. 447.

102. A. Brunner, *Geschichtlichkeit*, p. 157.
103. *Werke*, vol. 3, p. 30 (footnote).
104. ibid., pp. 20–1.
105. ibid., p. 28.
106. ibid., p. 21.
107. *Werke*, vol. 23, p. 536.
108. ibid., p. 511.
109. A. Schmidt, *Der Begriff der Natur in der Lehre von Marx*, p. 57.
110. cf. note 71.
111. K. Kautsky considers the human mind to be on the whole a conservative institution. (*Die materialistische Geschichtsauffassung*, vol. 1, p. 143.)
112. *Gespräche mit Georg Lukács*, p. 32–3.
113. M. Merleau-Ponty, *Humanismus und Terror*, vol. 2, 1966, p. 8.
114. *Werke*, vol. 23, p. 28.
115. *Werke*, vol. 1, p. 516.
116. W. I. Lenin, *Werke* (Dietz), 1961 f., vol. 1, p. 430–1.
117. *Werke*, vol. 38, p. 177–9.
118. *Werke*, vol. 1, p. 432.
119. cf. note 74.
120. cf. note 2.
121. T. W. Adorno, *Negative Dialektik*, pp. 313–15.
122. *Werke*, vol. 3, p. 27.
123. *Werke*, vol. 13, p. 9.
124. cf. also the corresponding passages in the *German Ideology*, *Werke*, vol. 3, pp. 35–7.
125. *Werke*, vol. 9, p. 226.
126. F. Mehring, *Über den historischen Materialismus*, 1947, p. 76.
127. cf. L. Trotsky, *Their Morals and Ours*.
128. F. Engels, *The Origin of the Family*, *Werke*, vol. 21, p. 97; Marx, *Critique of Political Economy*, p. 593.
129. F. Engels, *The Origin of the Family*, *Werke*, vol. 21, pp. 95–7, 152, and *Anti-Dühring*, *Werke*, vol. 20, p. 169.
130. 'Individuals have always acted by reason of their own motivations,' Marx writes in the *German Ideology* (*Werke*, vol. 3, p. 75). cf. also the following: 'In practice Communists treat . . . the conditions produced by previous production and traffic as inorganic, without for that reason imagining it was the plan or intention of previous generations to deliver them material, and without believing that those conditions were inorganic to the individuals who created them' (ibid., p. 71).
131. E. Bloch, *Naturrecht und menschliche Würde*, p. 219.
132. E. Bloch, *Das Prinzip Hoffnung*, pp. 274, 286.

133. ibid., p. 274, and other passages in the same chapter.
134. T. W. Adorno, *Negative Dialektik*, p. 272.
135. ibid., p. 312. cf. also the position taken by K. Kautsky, *Die materialistische Geschichtsauffassung*, vol. 2, pp. 769 ff.
136. *Gespräche mit Georg Lukács*, p. 108.
137. J. Habermas, *Theorie und Praxis*, pp. 179, 316, 310.
138. E. Topitsch, *Vom Ursprung und Ende der Metaphysik*, pp. 252-5.
139. *German Ideology*, *Werke*, vol. 3, p. 35. cf. also the following: 'The working class . . . has no ideals to realize; it has only to set free the elements of the new society that have already developed in the womb of collapsing bourgeois society.' *Werke*, vol. 17, p. 343.
140. *Das Ende der Utopie*, p. 58.
141. E. Kux, *Karl Marx: die revolutionäre Konfession*, 1967, pp. 96-7, 25.
142. The passage referred to occurs in volume three of *Capital* and reads as follows: 'The realm of freedom in fact begins at the point where the labour that is determined by need and external necessity ends; thus by the nature of things it lies beyond the sphere of real material production. . . . Freedom in this field can consist only in socialized humanity, the associated producers, rationally regulating this exchange of material with nature . . . accomplishing it with the minimum of expenditure of strength and in conditions worthiest and most adequate to their human nature. But it still remains a realm of necessity. Beyond it there begins the development of human strength that is an end in itself, the true realm of freedom which, however, can flourish only on the realm of necessity as its base' (*Werke*, vol. 25, p. 828).
143. In the introduction to *The Critique of Political Economy*, *Werke*, vol. 13, p. 9.
144. cf. W. F. Haug, '*Das Ganze und das ganz Andere*', *Antworten auf Herbert Marcuse*, 1968.
145. *Werke*, supplementary vol. 1, pp. 537-8.
146. *Werke*, vol. 3, pp. 74, 77.
147. *Werke*, vol. 4, p. 482.
148. *Werke*, supplementary vol. 1, p. 538.
149. G. Dicke, *Der Identitätsgedanke bei Feuerbach und Marx*, 1960, pp. 205-6.
150. G. Brunner, *Die Grundrechte im Sowjetsystem*, 1963, p. 74.
151. *Werke*, supplementary vol. 1, p. 539.
152. ibid., pp. 166-7.
153. *Werke*, vol. 4, p. 548.

154. cf. in particular, *Werke*, vol. 3, p. 67.

155. ibid., p. 70–7.

156. ibid., p. 70–1.

157. The following incident illustrates the strength of the tendency to attribute contempt for human individuality to Marxism. The author was once asked by a correspondent to verify a quotation attributed to Lenin according to which the latter said: 'There are no human beings, there is only a human mass.' The inquirer had heard these words attributed to Lenin in an address by the rector of the Philosophical-Theological University of Bamberg, and had himself quoted them in the meantime. It turned out, however, to be the result of an absurd mistranslation. Lenin had complained in a 1902 letter that a 'mass of people' were available for running illegal newspapers, but 'no people' able to do the job properly.

158. K. Löwith, *Weltgeschichte und Heilsgeschehen*, p. 48.

159. E. Topitsch, *Sozialphilosophie zwischen Ideologie und Wissenschaft*, 1966, p. 294.

160. R. Tucker, *Karl Marx*, p. 7.

161. As when the 'historical mission' of the proletariat is spoken of.

162. E. Topitsch, *Vom Ursprung und Ende der Metaphysik*, p. 255.

163. K. R. Popper, *Falsche Propheten. Hegel, Marx und die Folgen*, 1958, p. 104.

164. ibid., pp. 246–7.

165. ibid., p. 249.

166. ibid., pp. 108–9.

167. This idea appears in its most exaggerated form when the Marxist view of history is compared to a stream flowing past men which, as W. Theimer suggests (*Der Marxismus, Lehre – Wirkung – Kritik*, 1950, pp. 24–5), they can either watch or jump into.

168. M. Cornforth, *Dialectical Materialism. An introduction*, vol. 2, *Historical Materialism*, 1962, pp. 15–30.

169. F. Marek, *Philosophie der Weltrevolution*, 1966, pp. 15–24. In his book, *Die Gesellschaftslehre des sowjetischen Marxismus*, H. Marcuse also assumes a concept of history subject to objective laws that makes the same short-cut (pp. 23–6).

170. ibid., p. 23.

171. Quotations from I. Fetscher, *Der Marxismus: Seine Geschichte in Dokumenten*, vol. 1, 1962, pp. 420–5.

172. K. Vorländer, *Marx und Kant*, 1904, pp. 22–4. Repeated in *Kant und Marx*, 1925, p. 285.

173. M. Rubel, *Karl Marx, essai de biographie intellectuelle*, 1957.

174. P. Bigo, *Marxisme et Humanisme, introduction à l'œuvre économique de Karl Marx*, 1954.

175. I. Fetscher, *Karl Marx und der Marxismus*, 1967, p. 248.

176. L. Goldmann, *Dialektische Untersuchungen*, 1966, pp. 219–20.

177. L. Kofler, *Der proletarische Bürger*, p. 247.

178. V. I. Lenin, *Collected Works*, vol. 31, p. 293.

179. M. G. Zuravkov, 'Važnejšij princip kommunističeskoj morali' ('The most important principle of communist morality'), *Voprosy filosofii*, no. 5, 1963, p. 5.

180. W. P. Tugarinov, *Über die Werte des Lebens und der Kultur*, p. 16.

181. L. Goldmann, *Dialektische Untersuchungen*, p. 196.

182. ibid., pp. 235–6.

183. ibid., pp. 252–3.

184. cf. O. G. Drobnickij, *Mir oživšich predmetov. Problema cennosti i marksistkaja filosofia* ('The world of animated objects. The problem of values and Marxist philosophy'), 1967.

185. H. J. Lieber, *Philosophie, Soziologie, Gesellschaft*, 1965, pp. 182–3.

186. E. Bloch, *Philosophische Grundfragen I. Zur Ontologie des Noch-Nicht-Seins*, 1961, pp. 31–2.

187. E. Bloch, *Das Prinzip Hoffnung*, pp. 229–30.

188. E. Bloch, *Naturrecht und menschliche Würde*, pp. 223–5.

189. ibid., p. 225 (in almost literal agreement with a phrase in Lukács's essay on Moses Hess).

190. ibid., p. 2.

191. G. Hillmann (*Marx und Hegel: von der Spekulation zur Dialektik*, 1966) follows the development of Marx's thought from his early years, looking at it from the point of view of the various statements he made reflecting or depicting the development of his subjective attitude to 'objectivity'. We should like to suggest that wherever appropriate the term 'inter-subjectivity' should be substituted for 'objectivity'.

192. cf. the third of the *Theses on Feuerbach*. *Werke*, vol. 3, pp. 5–6.

193. M. Machoveč, 'Dialog als Menschlichkeit', *Neues Forum*, 1967, nos. 160–1, and continuation in following numbers.

194. L. Landgrebe, 'Das Problem der Dialektik,' Marxismusstudien, 3rd series, 1960, pp. 62–3. G. L. Kline ('Was Marx an Ethical Humanist?', *Akten des XIV Internationalen Kongresses für Philosophie*, 1968, pp. 69–73) similarly criticizes Marxist humanism as being an 'ideal humanism' related to the future that in the meantime grants the individual merely an instrumental value; he concludes that it is therefore not 'humanism in principle'.

195. K. Rahner, 'Christentum als Religion der absoluten Zukunft',

Christentum und Marxismus – Heute (Gespräche der Paulus-Gesellschaft, ed. E. Kellner), 1966, p. 210.

196. In a discussion on Rahner's paper, op. cit., p. 225.
197. W. Benjamin, *Zur Kritik der Gewalt*, 1965, p. 83.
198. The phrase 'The Marx of the law of history' is used by W. Koch in 'Geschichtsgesetz und Strategie bei Lenin', *Der Mensch im kommunistischen System (Tübinger Studien zur Geschichte und Politik)*, 1957, p. 42.
199. D. Del Vecchio, op. cit., p. 441, note 101.
200. T. W. Adorno, *Negative Dialektik*, pp. 313–14.
201. op. cit., p. 442. This critic misconstrues the primary determining function of the economic sphere as implying as the latter's temporal priority over the changes subordinate to it, as does B. Kopp, 'Die marxistische Theorie vom Überbau und Unterbau und ihre nicht-marxistischen Abwandlungen', *Zeitschrift für philosophische Forschung*, no. 4, 1968, pp. 577–8.
202. ibid., p. 313. Political authority in general is certainly economically conditioned (by the level of productivity attained). Marx is incidentally aware that political authority can itself be a factor in economic relations – as when he describes capital relations in the words of another author as 'command of labour' and regards it as an exception when such command over the labour of others acts 'not for the purpose of the exercise of authority but of private pleasure'.
203. op. cit., pp. 535–6.
204. This expression is used by Engels in a letter to G. Schmidt of 27 October 1890.
205. op. cit., p. 111, note 100.
206. K. Kautsky, *Die materialistische Geschichtsauffassung*, vol. 1, p. 6.
207. T. W. Adorno, *Negative Dialektik*, p. 315.
208. M. Adler, 'Grundlegung der materialistischen Geschichtsauffassung', *Soziologie des Marxismus* 1, 1964, p. 57.
209. op. cit., p. 43.
210. op. cit., p. 143.
211. op. cit., p. 149.
212. op. cit., p. 145.
213. cf. M. Bunge, *Causality. The Place of the Causal Principle in Modern Science*, 1959, pp. 49, 174.
214. *Grundlagen des Marxismus-Leninismus*, 1963, p. 157.
215. ibid., pp. 390, 392.
216. G. E. Glezermann, *O zakonach obscestvennogo razvitija*, ('On the laws of social development'), 1960, p. 148.

217. F. Marek, *Philosophie der Weltrevolution*, p. 19.

218. *Grundlagen des Marxismus-Leninismus*, pp. 157–64.

219. S. Warynski (pseudonym), *Die Wissenschaft von der Gesellschaft*, 1944, pp. 161–3.

220. E. Topitsch, *Vom Ursprung und Ende der Metaphysik*, pp. 262–3.

221. A. Brunner, *Geschichtlichkeit*, pp. 89–92.

222. J. Habermas, *Theorie und Praxis*, p. 189.

223. *Werke*, vol. 2, p. 38.

224. R. Luxemburg, *Ausgewählte Reden und Schriften*, vol. 2, 1955, p. 666.

225. N. Bukharin, *Theorie des historischen Materialismus*, 1922, p. 44.

226. A. Gramsci, *Philosophie der Praxis*, p. 204.

227. N. Janzen, in a lecture on 'Dialectics and their meaning for the construction of socialism', printed as a special supplement to *Die Presse der Sowjetunion*, no. 107, 1958, said: 'To us, who are constructing socialism, the objective conformity with natural law of the development of human society is an especially gratifying fact. On the basis of this conformity with law we know that one form of society succeeds another . . . just as inevitably and in accordance with natural law as spring follows winter and summer spring . . . and that capitalist society is eventually succeeded by communism.'

228. Apart from occasional hints (e.g., by V. P. Tugarinov in a work that appeared in 1956), Soviet Marxist philosophers have done little to promote consciousness of this difference. An attempt to remedy this notorious deficiency is made in O. I. Dzoiiev's *Priroda istoričeskoj neobchodimosti* ('The nature of historical necessity'), 1967. He sets out to define the share of free choice and its axiological determination in history.

229. G. W. Plekhanov, *Über die Rolle der Persönlichkeit in der Geschichte*, 1945, pp. 11–12.

230. E. Topitsch, *Vom Ursprung und Ende der Metaphysik*, p. 261.

231. G. Lukács, *Geschichte und Klassenbewusstsein*, pp. 308–13.

232. *Werke*, vol. 20, p. 106.

233. *Werke*, vol. 4, p. 363.

234. In a letter to J. Weydemeyer of 5 March 1852, *Werke*, vol. 28, p. 508.

235. In a letter to H. Schlüter of 14 June 1890.

236. *Werke*, vol. 17, p. 278.

237. The following is quoted from a publicist's summing up: 'But in the west Marx's calculation did not work out. Capital has not gained control of the state. It has not made the rich richer and the poor poorer. Capitalism has led the workers, not to im-

poverishment, but to a previously unimagined high standard of living, to full employment instead of to the "industrial reserve army" of the unemployed. The middle class, instead of being crushed between the capitalists and the proletariat, has powerfully expanded in both directions. Concentration has not ended in monopoly capitalism, and capital accumulation has not gone to the benefit of a few capitalists, but to undertakings that emancipated themselves from capital and widely distributed their property. Capitalism no longer staggers from crisis to crisis; since the low point of 1930 it has consolidated itself and gone forward to fresh developments. . . . In Marx's time capitalism was in its puberty, but now it has reached the adult stage. Then it behaved as a wild beast of prey, now it has been domesticated.' (J. Gaitanides, 'Volkskapitalismus – Romantik oder Realität?', *Aus Politik und Zeitgeschichte*, supplemented to the weekly *Das Parlament*, 20 November 1957.

238. *Werke*, vol. 8, p. 118.
239. A. Gramsci, *Philosophie der Praxis*, p. 24.
240. *Werke*, vol. 3, pp. 34–5.
241. In a letter to L. Kugelmann of 17 April 1871, *Werke*, vol. 33, p. 109.
242. In 'Our Revolution' (1923) one of Lenin's last statements, *Collected Works*, vol. 33, pp. 478–9.
243. The balance of probability is that at least a strict military dictatorship, possibly a variety of Fascism, might have been established. What is possible after a frustrated revolution was demonstrated in Germany.
244. I. Deutscher, *The Unfinished Revolution, 1917–1967*, 1967, p. 9.
245. ibid., pp. 38, 41.
246. ibid., p. 55. E. Mandel, *Marxistische Wirtschaftstheorie*, p. 660 ff., discusses in detail the basic economic theory of 'developmental necessities', the necessity of forced accumulation, and comes to the conclusion that better results could have been achieved at smaller cost to the workers.
247. op. cit., p. 85.
248. Lenin, *Werke*, vol. 1, p. 414, Marx/Engels, *Werke*, vol. 3, p. 40, footnote.

Index

DATE DUE

F			
FE 15 '77			
AP 7'78			
29 8			